A Spenser Chronology

Willy Maley

Lecturer, Department of English
Queen Mary and Westfield College
University of London

M

Barnes & Noble Books

First published in Great Britain 1994 by
THE MACMILLAN PRESS LTD
Houndmills, Basingstoke, Hampshire RG21 2XS
and London
Companies and representatives
throughout the world

This book is published in Macmillan's *Author Chronologies* series

A catalogue record for this book is available
from the British Library.

ISBN 0–333–53744–0

Printed in Great Britain by
Antony Rowe Ltd
Chippenham, Wiltshire

First published in the United States of America 1994 by
BARNES & NOBLE BOOKS
4720 Boston Way
Lanham, MD 20706

Library of Congress Cataloging-in-Publication Data
Maley, Willy.
A Spenser chronology / Willy Maley.
p.   cm.
Includes bibliographical references and index.
ISBN 0–389–21010–2
1. Spenser, Edmund.   1552?–1599—Chronology.   I. Title.
PR2363.M35   1994
821'.3—dc20
                                                     93–2456
                                                       CIP

A SPENSER CHRONOLOGY

For Geraldine

Contents

General Editor's Preface

Most biographies are ill adapted to serve as works of reference – not surprisingly so, since the biographer is likely to regard his function as the devising of a continuous and readable narrative, with excursions into interpretation and speculation, rather than a bald recital of facts. There are times, however, when anyone reading for business or pleasure needs to check a point quickly or to obtain a rapid overview of part of an author's life or career, and at such moments turning over the pages of a biography can be a time-consuming and frustrating occupation. The present series of volumes aims at providing a means whereby the chronological facts of an author's life and career, rather than needing to be prised out of the narrative in which they are (if they appear at all) securely embedded, can be seen at a glance. Moreover, whereas biographies are often, and quite understandably, vague over matters of fact (since it makes for tediousness to be forever enumerating details of dates and places), a chronology can be precise whenever it is possible to be precise.

Thanks to the survival, sometimes in very large quantities, of letters, diaries, notebooks and other documents, as well as to thoroughly researched biographies and bibliographies, this material now exists in abundance for many major authors. In the case of, for example, Dickens, we can often ascertain what he was doing in each month and week, and almost on each day, of his prodigiously active working life; and the student of, say, *David Copperfield* is likely to find it fascinating as well as useful to know just when Dickens was at work on each part of that novel, what other literary enterprises he was engaged in at the same time, whom he was meeting, what places he was visiting and what were the relevant circumstances of his personal and professional life. Such a chronology is not, of course, a substitute for a biography; but its arrangement, in combination with its index, makes it a much more convenient tool for this kind of purpose; and it may be acceptable as a form of 'alternative' biography, with its own distinctive advantages as well as its obvious limitations.

Since information relating to an author's early years is usually scanty and chronologically imprecise, the opening section of some volumes in this series groups together the years of childhood and adolescence. Thereafter each year, and usually each month, is dealt with separately. Information not readily assignable to a specific month or day is given as a general note under the relevant year or month. The first entry for each month carries an indication of the day of the week, so that when necessary this can be readily calculated for other dates. Each volume also contains a bibliography of the principal sources of information. In the chronology itself, the sources of many of the more specific items, including quotations, are identified, in order that the reader who wishes to do so may consult the original contexts.

NORMAN PAGE

Acknowledgements

Thanks to Professor Lisa Jardine, my Ph.D. supervisor, for early encouragement and inspiration. Dr Andrew Hadfield and Professor Jean Brink read through the typescript after it had gone to press and made some useful suggestions that I tried to incorporate at proof stage. I thank them for their advice and support. All errors and oversights remain my own: 'God helpe the man so wrapt in *Errours* endlesse traine.'

List of Abbreviations

I have retained the original spelling in quoting from all primary sources, although 'u', 'v', 'i' and 'j' have been normalised.

Titles of Spenser's works are abbreviated as follows:

Am.	*Amoretti*
As.	*Astrophel*
Bel.	*Visions of Bellay*
Col.	*Colin Clouts Come Home Againe*
Comp.	*Complaints*
Daph.	*Daphnaida*
Epith.	*Epithalamion*
FQ	*Faerie Queene*
Gn.	*Virgils Gnat*
HL	*Hymne in Honour of Love*
HB	*Hymne in Honour of Beautie*
HHL	*Hymne of Heavenlie Love*
MHT	*Mother Hubberds Tale*
Mui.	*Muipotmos*
Pet.	*Visions of Petrarch*
Proth.	*Prothalamion*
RR	*Ruines of Rome*
RT	*Ruines of Time*
SC	*Shepheardes Calender*
TM	*Teares of the Muses*
Van.	*Visions of the Worlds Vanitie*

Other abbreviations

BL	British Library, London
CSPI	*Calender of State Papers, Ireland*
CSPF	*Calender of State Papers, Foreign*
CSPS	*Calender of State Papers, Scotland*
Fiants	*Calendar of Fiants for the reign of Elizabeth*, London

PRO   Public Record Office, London
STC   A. W. Pollard and G. R. Redgrave, *Short-Title Catalogue of Books Printed in England* . . . *1475–1640* (1926, also 1946)
Variorum   *The Works of Edmund Spenser: A Variorum Edition*, ed. Greenlaw *et al.*, 10 vols (Baltimore, 1932–49)

Introduction

Edmund Spenser is one of the most crucial literary figures of the English Renaissance, a writer who, in addition to stimulating a whole contemporary pastoral tradition, posthumously exerted a powerful influence upon a series of major canonical authors, including Milton, Blake and Eliot. Despite the number of specialist monographs on the poet, and the commendable biography undertaken by A. C. Judson for the *Variorum* edition of his works, a major gap remains in Spenser studies. This gap arises from the lack of a proper synthesis of the literary life of Spenser – viewed through his early relations with the Sidney–Leicester circle at court – and the historical life of Spenser – considered in terms of concrete detail regarding his career as a planter and administrator in Ireland.

By bringing together these two strands of scholarship on Spenser, splicing the English Renaissance literary biography with the early modern Irish historiography, one can reconstruct a fuller picture of the poet than has hitherto been available. Furthermore, this new portrait of Spenser will appeal across two disciplines – English and History – by being both a biographical text on a major canonical author, and an historical work outlining the career of an influential Elizabethan planter.

The juxtaposition of events, publications, and themes in Elizabethan Irish historiography with those in contemporary English society will provide the reader of Spenser for the first time with a comprehensive guide to Faeryland and Ireland. Spenser's life coincides with a watershed in Anglo-Irish relations, and the configuration of Spenser's Cambridge intellectual preparation, court patronage, colonial politics and eventual dislodging from the Irish landscape can be charted alongside the English government's unsuccessful efforts at imposing the reformation in Ireland by peaceful means, and in a piecemeal manner. Spenser spent almost his entire literary career in Ireland, and his knowledge of that country was intimate. His knowledge stretched far beyond his Kilcolman estate. Carpenter, for example, divides Spenser's life in Ireland into three distinct parts: in 1580–6, he was chiefly in or near

Dublin; 1586–98, chiefly at Kilcolman; 1589–90, 1595–7 and 1598–9 encompass visits to England.

There are a number of key biographies and reference books that attempt to shed light on the life of Spenser. F. I. Carpenter's *Reference Guide* (1923), Pauline Henley's *Spenser in Ireland* (1928), the *Variorum* edition of Spenser's works, including A. C. Judson's authoritative biography (1945), and H. S. V. Jones's *Spenser Handbook* (1930) are among the most notable. The publication of *The Spenser Encyclopedia* is certainly a significant landmark in Spenser studies, but it is an unwieldy text for the scholar in search of a factual account of the poet's life.

Spenser's biographers have always been aware of the paucity of materials relating directly to Spenser's activities, experiences and whereabouts during the course of his life. J. P. Collier declared: 'Few things are more difficult than to settle, at all satisfactorily, matters relating to chronology in Spenser's life and writings.'

G. C. Craik observed: 'The biography of Spenser is to a great extent a series of assumptions, or of assertions, repeated by one writer after another, but resting originally upon little or no evidence.' In the Preface to his *Variorum* biography of Spenser, Judson defended his project thus: 'The present life differs from most of its predecessors in the attention given to the atmosphere in which Spenser moved. I have undertaken to place him in his environment, surround him with his friends and associates, and study the influences both physical and human upon him.'

Conyers Read, reviewing Judson's efforts, questioned the scholarly basis of his biographical enterprise: 'Outside of what Edmund Spenser himself wrote all that is positively known about his life could probably be written in a few short paragraphs. The rest is inference, surmise, and conjecture.'

In comparison with preceding chronologies of modern authors, this volume is lacking in day-to-day material, but it does give a clearer picture of Spenser's whereabouts and activities than has hitherto been available.* I have tried, as far as possible, to abjure

---

* For previous attempts at chronologies of Spenser's life, see 'Chronological Outline of the Life', in F. I. Carpenter (1923) pp. 11–21; 'Chronological Table of Spenser's Life and Principal Publications', in A. C. Hamilton (ed.), *Spenser: The Faerie Queene* (London and New York: Longman, 1977) pp. viii–xii; and the 'Chronology' in Simon Shepherd, *Spenser* (Brighton: Harvester Wheatsheaf, 1989) pp. 120–3.

'inference, surmise, and conjecture', but instead have anticipated a set of questions. What exactly did Spenser do in Ireland? What were his regular activities and duties outside of writing *The Faerie Queene*? Where was he at a particular time? How much travelling did he do? Who were his acquaintances?

This *Spenser Chronology* tries to fill in the large factual gaps that have always been felt to exist in Spenser scholarship. It registers appointments, records events and lists publications. The Irish historical material is compiled principally from two sources, Steven G. Ellis, *Tudor Ireland* (1985) pp. 1–11, and Moody, Martin and Byrne (eds), *Early Modern Ireland* (1982) pp. 195–253. I have highlighted those historical incidents and literary landmarks most relevant to Spenser.

No reference work is exhaustive. This *Chronology* remains 'unperfite', awaiting further research. Spenser's own historical method was first of all to consult with the available chronicles and official histories:

> But unto them besides I add myne own readinge and out of them bothe togeather with comparison of times likenes of manners and Customes Affinytie of wordes and names properties of natures and uses resemblaunces of rights and Ceremonies monimentes of Churches and Tombes and many other like circumstances I doe gather a likelyhode of truethe, not certainly affirminge anye thinge but by Conferringe of times nacions languages monimentes and such like I doe hunte out a probabilitye of things which I doe leave unto your judgement to beleeve or refuse. (*View*, 1208–15)

I hope that readers of this *Chronology* learn more about the life and work of Spenser from the 'Conferringe of times' that it offers.

A Spenser Chronology

Early Years (?1552–76)

1552–4 S born, probably in London, the family possibly originating in Lancashire.

1553 (2 Feb) John Bale consecrated bishop of Ossory. First of many English radical Protestant clerics to arrive in Ireland.
(6 July) Death of Edward VI.
(27 July) Proclamation in Ireland of Lady Jane Grey as queen.
(20 Aug) Proclamation in Ireland of Mary I. Bale departs diocese.

1554 (13 May) Gerald Fitzgerald created 11th earl of Kildare.

1555 (7 June) Bull of Pope Paul IV making Ireland a kingdom.

1556 (13 Apr) Sir Henry Sidney's first Irish appointment, as undertreasurer.
(26 May) Thomas Radcliffe, Lord Fitzwalter sworn in as Lord Deputy.

1557 (17 Feb) Radcliffe becomes earl of Sussex.
(1 June–2 July) Parliament in Dublin passes legislation to undertake Leix-Offaly plantation, and establish Queen's and King's Counties.

1558 (7 Jan) Loss of English pale around Calais to French.
(17 Nov) Death of Mary I and accession of Elizabeth I.
(12 Dec) Sidney promoted to Lord Justice.

1560 (11/12 Jan–1 Feb) Sussex's second parliament in Dublin passes acts of supremacy and uniformity.

1561 (20 Sep) The Guild of Merchant Taylors founds Merchant Taylors' School, housed in an old mansion called the Manor of the Rose, in the parish of St Lawrence-Pountney. Formally constituted on the 24th of this month. Statutes stipulate that the maximum number of pupils is 250, comprising 100 poor men's sons, who

1

make no parental contribution, 50 others at half fee of 5 shillings a quarter, and 100 'rich or mean men's children'. S enters Merchant Taylor's School as a 'poor scholar', where he remains for eight years. Headmaster is classical scholar and educational theorist Richard Mulcaster, an eloquent advocate of the English language who none the less recognised the necessity of augmenting it with borrowings from other tongues. Among fellow students are Thomas Kyd, Lancelot Andrewes and Thomas Lodge. The schoolday begins at 7 a.m. summer and winter, and ends at 5 p.m., with an intermission from 11 a.m. to 1 p.m. During his time at Merchant Taylors', S receives a gown from the Robert Nowell bequest.

1562   (6 Jan) Shane O'Neill submits to Elizabeth at Whitehall.

(3 July) Order for establishment of court of castle chamber in Ireland.

(16 Aug) First visitation to Merchant Taylors' by Grindal, Nowell and Watts.

1563   (April) Sussex campaigns against Shane O'Neill.

(11 Sep) O'Neill submits.

Publication of Barnaby Googe's *Eglogs, Epytaphs and Sonettes*, London.

1564   (12 Mar) A son of Mulcaster christened Sylvanus in St Lawrence Pountney, the parish church of Merchant Taylors'.

(13 Nov) At eight o'clock this morning, S and other pupils at Merchant Taylors' present themselves before a board of examiners, including Miles Coverdale, renowned for his work on the translation of the English bible. After 'a pythe and eloquent oration in the midst of the school' by a boy named King, S may have been amongst those pupils who presented copies of verses and epistles to Bishop Grindal, later praised as 'Algrind' in *SC*. Also present was Alexander Nowell, Dean of St Paul's, described as 'a learned man and charitable to the poor, especially if they had anything of the scholar in them'. The Dean's brother, Robert Nowell, had established a fund for poor scholars, of which S was a beneficiary both at school and on going up to Cambridge. It is worth noting that Lawrence, another of the Nowell brothers, antiquary and Dean of Lichfield, had a map of Ireland made before his death in

1576. This may have been one of the maps S had access to before and during his Irish sojourn.

1565 (13 Oct) Sidney elevated to Lord Deputy of Ireland, the first of three terms in this office.

(12 Nov) Third visitation to Merchant Taylors', including Thomas Watts.

1566 (Sep–12 Nov) Henry Sidney campaigns in Ulster.

1567 (2 June) Death of Shane O'Neill.

(24 July) Accession of James VI.

(9 Oct) Robert Weston and William Fitzwilliam made Justices of Ireland.

Cartographer Robert Lythe in Ireland.

1568 (17 Apr) Henry Sidney reappointed Lord Deputy of Ireland.

1569 (6 Feb) Robert Nowell, of Gray's Inn, prominent London lawyer, dies. S gets a gown, as do five other pupils of Merchant Taylors', on the occasion of Nowell's funeral. Dean Alexander Nowell was trustee of his brother's estate, and a book of disbursements was kept by his steward James Wotton. S subsequently receives several payments from the Nowell fund.

(11 Mar) Attainder of Shane O'Neill.

(20 Mar) Licence granted to John Hooker to print Irish statutes.

(28 Apr) S arrives in Cambridge, and receives 10 shillings from the Robert Nowell bequest.

(20 May) S admitted as sizar (a poor scholar given servant's duties) to Pembroke Hall, Cambridge. 'Sizar' comes from 'size', a portion of bread and ale which the poor student had free. There were around 100 persons at Pembroke when S matriculated. On the academic side there was the master, twenty-four major fellows, six minor fellows, seven inferior ministers (servants), thirty-six pensioners (paying students) and thirteen sizars – poor scholars.

(22 July) Jan van der Noot's *Theatre for Worldlings* entered in Stationers' Register by Henry Bynneman.

(July–Sep) Desmond-Butler Revolt.

(18 Oct) Humphrey Gilbert appointed colonel of Munster.

Bill signed to one 'Edmonde Spencer' as bearer from Tours of letters from Sir Henry Norris, English ambassador to France, to

Elizabeth: 'Payde upon a bill signed by Mr Secretarye dated at Wyndsor xviij° Octobris 1569 To Edmonde Spencer that broughte lres to the Quenes Ma^{tis} from Sir Henrye Norrys knighte her Ma^{ts} Embassador in Fraunce beinge then at Towars in the sayde Realme, for his charges the some of vj^{li}.xiij^s.iiij^d. over and besydes ix^{li}. prested to hym by Sir Henrye Norrys'.

(Nov/Dec) James Spenser, possibly a relative of S's, is serving as Master of the Ordnance in Ireland.

Edmund Campion is in Dublin, a guest of the Stanyhursts. S publishes anonymously translations of 'Visions of Petrarch' and 'Visions of du Bellay', in *A theatre for Worldlings*, compiled by the Dutch Calvinist, Jan van der Noot, and published by Henry Bynneman.

1570 (25 Feb) Excommunication of Elizabeth.

(19 Aug) Elizabeth writes to her Irish viceroy, Sir Henry Sidney, declining his request that his sixteen-year-old son, Philip, join him in Ireland, on the grounds that the plague is prevalent there.

(7 Nov) S paid 6 shillings from the Nowell bequest.

Beginning of S's friendship with Gabriel Harvey, newly appointed Fellow of Pembroke.

1571 There is a John Spenser at Merchant Taylors' School this year, but there is as yet no evidence that he was a relation of S. This may be the same John Spenser who matriculated as a Sizar at Pembroke in Easter 1575, and took his BA in 1577–8. A John Spenser was serving as Constable of Limerick in 1579. If these three are one and the same, the striking parallels with S's career lend weight to the conjecture that John Spenser was S's brother.

About this time, Gabriel Harvey is involved in a debate at Hill Hall, Theydon Mount, centre of the Smith family estate. Among the participants in a discussion of classical precedents for colonial projects are Thomas Smith junior, Sir Humphrey Gilbert, Sir Thomas Smith, Dr Walter Haddon, John Wood 'and several others of gentle birth': 'Thomas Smith junior and Sir Humphrey Gilbert [debated] for Marcellus, Thomas Smith senior and Doctor Walter Haddon for Fabius Maximus, before an audience at Hill Hall consisting at that very time of myself, John Wood, and several others of gentle birth. At length the son and Sir Humphrey yielded to the distinguished Secretary: I am not sure that Marcellus yielded to Fabius. Both of them worthy, and judicious. Marcellus the more powerful; Fabius the more cunning. Neither was the latter un-prepared [weak], nor the former imprudent, each as indispensable as the other in his place. There are times when I would rather be Marcellus, times when Fabius.' In *Foure Letters*, 1592, Harvey refers to 'my Cosen, M. Thomas Smith . . . Colonel of the Ards in Ireland'. Since the early 1570s are the period of S's closest in-volvement with Harvey, the Smith debate, recorded by Harvey in Latin marginal notes to his copy of Livy's *Decades*, suggests a much earlier acquaintance with Irish affairs on the part of S than has hitherto been appreciated. S mentions Smith and Harvey together in the gloss of 'couthe' in *SC Jan*.

(24 Apr) S paid 2 shillings and sixpence from Nowell bequest.

(16 Nov) Sir Thomas Smith and his son, Thomas, granted lands in Clandeboye and the Ards.

(11 Dec) Sir William Fitzwilliam appointed Lord Deputy of Ireland.

Between now and 1574 S apparently receives five payments, allegedly for ill-health, from Pembroke. It is not clear – to me at least – exactly what these payments were for or what their relationship, if any, is to the Nowell bequest payments (see Watson, 1992, pp. 6–7; see entry under 16 Oct 1574).

1572 (*c*.31 May) Campion leaves Ireland.

(24 Aug) St Bartholomew's day massacre in Paris.

(31 Aug) Thomas Smith (junior), son of Sir Thomas Smith, lands with *c*.100 colonists at Strangford Lough.

1573 (17 July) Walter Devereux sails for Ireland.

(Aug) Walter Devereux, first earl of Essex, arrives at Carrickfergus to plant Antrim.

(18 Oct) Smith junior killed in the Ards.

S graduates BA, eleventh in a list of 120.

1574 (10 Oct) S receives four 'aegrotat' (he is sick) payments for the last six weeks of college year, extended to 10 Oct (see Attwater, 1936). These payments do not necessarily imply that S was sick.

1575 (26 July) Rathlin Island massacre. Captains Francis Drake and John Norris, under orders from the Earl of Essex, lead slaughter of 600 Scots.

(5 Aug) Henry Sidney reappointed Lord Deputy.

1576   Lawrence Nowell's map of Ireland – *MS Abbreviate of Ireland and Description of the Power of Irishmen* – is in circulation by this year.

(10 Jan) Edmund Grindal appointed Archbishop of Canterbury.

(9 Mar) First earl of Essex made earl marshal of Ireland.

(23 Apr) William Gerrard appointed Lord Chancellor.

(20 June) Sir William Drury appointed president of Munster.

(26 June) Grace passed for MA. S graduates MA, sixty-sixth in a list of seventy.

(23 July) Nicholas Malby installed as military governor of Connaught.

(22 Sep) Essex dies in Dublin. Philip Sidney, in Mayo with his father, on hearing of Essex's illness had hurried to Dublin, but found the earl dead on his arrival.

(20 Dec) Archbishop Grindal refuses to curtail 'prophesyings' and tells Elizabeth that she is 'a mortal creature'.

Some speculation that S travelled to the 'Northparts', possibly the family home in Lancashire, around this time, where he had a love affair with 'Rosalind', hinted at by E. K. in the gloss to *SC Jun*.

1577

February
1   Barnaby Googe's *Fowre Bookes of Husbandrie*, published in 1582, dated from Kingstown in Ireland, and dedicated to Sir William Fitzwilliam.

June
Archbishop Grindal is suspended for non-compliance with the ban on prophesyings.

July
1   S in Ireland, possibly as bearer of letters from the earl of Leicester to Sir Henry Sidney and Sir William Drury, where he witnesses the execution of Murrogh O'Brien at Limerick, recorded in *View*, where Irenius says 'at the execucion of A notable Traitour at Limericke Called murrogh Obrien I sawe an olde woman which was his foster mother take up his heade whilste he was quartered and sucked up all the blodd runninge theareout Sayinge that the earth was not worthie to

drinke it and thearewith allso steped her face, and breste and torne heare Cryinge and shrikinge out moste terrible' (1937–42). Sir William Drury justified the execution thus: 'the ferste day off thys moneth I adjorned the sesstyons for thys cowntie off lymeryke, untill a nu warnyng, and have caused one murough o bryen a second piller off Jemes fitz morisch is late rebellyon and a praktyser off thys nue combination a man off no less fame then James hym selfe) beyng orderly Indited arraygned condempned & Judged for late offences wythyn these iiij monethes (because I woold not seame to unrypp old matters) to be ther executed thre hundered powndes was offered for hys lyfe and more woold have been geven but thre thousands choold not have saved hym/thearle of dessemond made greate acompte of hym and so did all the discontentid for he was a fyte Instrument to execute an evell enterpryse, he was amongest the people In greate extymation he was holden the best & forwardest horseman off Ireland/he was greatly off the good feared hys dethe was farre better then hys lyffe, and he confessed he had deserved dethe.' S may have functioned for a time as Lord Deputy Sidney's private secretary, in the same way that he later served Lord Grey.

8   S possibly back in London bearing letters for Leicester from Drury, together with a 'cast of falcons of the best eyrie in this province' (*Cal. of Carew MSS.*, 1575–88, p. 104).

c.September
Philip Sidney writes *Discourse of Irish Affairs*.

November/December
Massacre by English soldiers of O'Connors and O'Mores at Mullaghmast, Co. Kildare.

December
Publication of Holinshed's *Chronicles*.

1578

January
Philip Sidney presents his *Discourse of Irish Affairs* to Elizabeth.

April
1   Dr John Young, former Master of Pembroke Hall, consecrated
    Bishop of Rochester in Kent by Archbishop Grindal. From
    about this time, S serves as Young's secretary. Young's official
    residence is at Bromley in Kent, ten miles from London.
27 Sir William Drury appointed Justice of Ireland.

June
16 John Derricke's *Image of Irelande*, published in 1581, dated from
    Dublin, and dedicated to Philip Sidney.
25 Thomas Stukeley's papal expedition leaves Lisbon for Ireland
    in two ships. Stukeley, most of the Italian forces, and both
    captains are lost at sea. Only forty survive.

September
12 Henry Sidney leaves Ireland for the last time.
14 Sir William Drury sworn in as Lord Justice.

November
23 S makes out rental receipt as secretary to Bishop Young
    (University of Kansas, uncatalogued manuscript, North
    2C:2:1).

December
20 S with Harvey in London, presenting him with four 'foolish
    bookes' – *Howleglas, Scoggin, Skelton* and *Lazarillo*. S described
    by Harvey as a 'young Italianate signor and French monsieur'.
    S tells Harvey he must read all four texts by 1 January or give
    him his four volumes of Lucian in return. S also presents
    Harvey with a piece of travel literature, a copy of Jerome
    Turler's *The Traveiler . . . devided into two Bookes. The first
    conteyning a notable discourse of the maner and order of traveiling
    oversea, or into strange and forein Countreys. The second
    comprehending an excellent description of the most delicious Realme
    of Naples in Italy*, published in 1575, inscribed: 'Gabrielis
    Harveij'. 'ex dono Spenserii, Episcopi Roffensis Secretarii.
    1578' (A gift of Edmund Spenser, secretary of the Bishop of
    Rochester). The bottom of the final page reads: 'Legi pridie
    Cal. Decembrus. 1578. Gabriel Harvey.'

1579

March
31 Elizabeth presents 'a newe establishment' for Ireland, detailing monies due to her servants there, including S's future associate, Lodowick Bryskett: '*Necessaries* for Lodovicke Bryskett, clerk of the Councell and the Lord Justice secretarie, not to exceed xxx^{li} sterling per annum, makinge Irishe xl^{li}.'

April
10 Date of Prefatory Epistle to *SC* by E. K. Signed 'Immerito' (the unworthy) and dedicated to Philip Sidney. Possibly penned by Edward Kirke, but identification remains uncertain. S may have written some of *Hub.* at this time. S had begun *FQ*. E. K. refers to some 'lost' works – *Dreames*, with commentary and illustrations, praised by Harvey for 'that singular extra-ordinarie veine and invention' found in the best Greek and Italian writers, *Legendes*, *Courte of Cupide* (possibly revised in *FQ* III xi–xii, VI vii), a translation of Moschus's *Idyllion of Wandring Love* (perhaps from Politian's Latin version), *Pageaunts*, *The Englishe Poete* (a theoretical tract that would correlate with the second part of Philip Sidney's *Apology for Poetry*), and *Sonnets*.

July
10 S back in London, according to Harvey, suggesting end of his secretaryship under Young.
28 William Gerrard, the Lord Chancellor, writes to the earl of Leicester from Dublin, advising him of the movements of Pelham, the Lord Justice, and promising to keep him availed of the Irish situation.

October
5 S enters service of earl of Leicester as confidential emissary, and writes to Harvey from 'Leycester House' of his intentions to go abroad on his patron's orders.
11 Sir William Pelham elected Lord Justice of Ireland by Privy Council. Sir Warham St Leger – uncle of the Captain Warham St Leger present in Bryskett's house at the literary gatherings early in 1582 – appointed provost marshal of Munster 'with the fee of two shillings sterling a day'.

15–16 S writes to Harvey from Westminster that he is in 'some use of familiarity' with Philip Sidney and Edward Dyer, discussing with them a classical reform of English metre that will bring 'a generall surceasing and silence of balde Rymers'.

16 Lord Justice Pelham writes from Limerick to Sir Francis Walsingham: 'Lord Justice Pelham to Walsyngham. Death of the late Lord Justice. His election. The wants to be declared by the Lord Chancellor to be supplied. Gerrarde to be comforted by some large portion of Her Majesty's favour. His brother Spenser to solicit his affairs.' This is possibly a reference to James Spenser, or to John Spenser, constable of Limerick.

23 Harvey writes to S from Trinity Hall, Cambridge, telling him that 'you shall not, I saye, bee gone over Sea, for al your saying, neither the next nor the nexte weeke'.

27 An 'Edmounde Spenser', probably the poet, marries Maccabaeus Chylde at St Margaret's, Westminster. Two children: Sylvanus (perhaps after Mulcaster's son) and Catherine.

November
2 Earl of Desmond proclaimed traitor.
6 Lord Justice Pelham issues 'A proclamation that every horsmane should were redd Crosses':

By the lo: Justice
William Pelham

fforasmuch as the said lo: Justice expresse pleasure is, that all horsemen that are to intende her Ma^{tis}: service in this assemblid Armie, shalbe knowne from others: Not beinge of the same retinewe his lo: ordereth, publisheth, and Comandeth in her Ma^{tis}: Name, that all the said horsemen both Englishe and Irishe, shall presentlie provide in redines two rede crosses, either of Silke or Cloth, the one to be fastened on the breste, and the other on the backe of Eache such horseman as is usuall, and to conteyne in lenght viij inches, and in bredthe one Inche, and a halfe, to be Worne upon every horsemans uppermoste garment wch he purposeth to serve in, be it habergine, Jacke or other upper garment, for defence, What so ever upon paine for not havinge such a crosse, as is before mentioned by

Wensdaie morninge next, eache horseman to forfaicte xx^s, & that the provoste Marshall of her Ma^{tis}: Armie shall leavie, and take upp eache such forfaiture to be disposed at the pleasure of the said lo: Justice Yeven at Limiricke the vj Novembr 1579. (*Cal. Carew MSS.*, 1575–88, no. 154, pp. 166–7).

This proclamation possibly inspired S's Redcrosse Knight in *FQ*.

23 A group of privy councillors, including the earl of Leicester, 'appointed by her majesty's special commandment to consult of the affairs of Ireland'. S was a possible courier this month, carrying letters from London to Limerick for the Lord Justice, Sir William Pelham. John Spenser, possibly a relative of S, installed as constable of Limerick at this time.

December
5 S's *SC* entered in Stationers' Register.

1580

March
1 Prerogative Court Ecclesiastical established in Ireland.

April
1 Sir Henry Wallop writes to Lord Burghley from Limerick referring to 'his [i.e. Burghley's] letters of March 6 by James Spenser', possibly a relative of S (*CSPI* 72.30).
2 S writes to Harvey from Westminster. Tells Harvey he 'wil in hand forthwith with my *Faery Queene*'.
7 Harvey writes to S from Cambridge, criticising intellectual fashions there.

In another of Harvey's letters he offers an alternative rendition of Willy and Thomalin's emblems for *SC March*. This letter is undated but belongs with this month's correspondence.

One portion of *FQ* described by Harvey during this month as '*Hobgoblin* runne away with the Garland from *Apollo*'.

June

19 S–Harvey correspondence, *Three Proper, and wittie, familiar letters*, has its address 'To the Curteous Buyer' dated this day 'by a Welwiller of the two Authors'.

30 S–Harvey Letters entered in Stationers' Register.

July

14 Pelham sues again for 'furtherance for his brother Spencer's suits'. Pelham writes from Limerick (*CSPI* 74.233.28): 'Lord Justice Pelham to Walsyngham. The correction of Desmond and his favourer the Viscount Barry to be an example of terror. Fenton Secretary. Pelham to compound the matter with Mr. Bellewe. Furtherance for his brother Spencer's suits. His diligence in the war. Plat for Munster. Peril in restoring the urraghs to Turlough Lynagh. Fulk Greville hurt in the leg.'

15 Arthur, Lord Grey de Wilton, appointed Lord Deputy of Ireland. Don Jacop (James) 'Gherardini', an Irishman, together with Alexander Bertoni, leaves Lisbon for Ireland. Landing at Smerwick, they disembark and establish fortifications. 'Gherardini' is killed in skirmishes with the English.

29 Pelham reports from Limerick (*CSPI* 74.75): 'Lord Justice Pelham to Walsyngham. Has received 10 letters since the despatch of his brother Spenser. Has set the Spaniards at Cork at liberty. Friendship to the Bishop of Ossory. Friendship to the Chancellor. Willing to serve under Lord Grey. The starting of the Pale cannot long keep Desmond upright. Sir W. Sentleger the author of the device to coop up the loose Lords. If the foreign aid come, few will stick with Her Majesty. Sir L. Dillon most faithful. 80 sail of well appointed ships expected. Arrival of victuals. Want of coals, horse shoes and nails.'

S appointed secretary to the Lord Deputy, paid at a rate of £10 half-yearly.

August

c.10 The new viceroy leaves Beaumaris for Ireland.

12 Grey arrives in Dublin aboard the *Handmaid*, captained by George Thornton, and assumes residence at Dublin Castle.

25 Grey defeated by O'Byrne at Glenmalure.

28 Sebastiano de San Guiseppe, colonel and general of papal force, leaves Santo Ander at the head of an Armada.

29 Copy of letter in hand of S, Sir Hugh Magennis to Grey, Narrow Water, near Newry (*CSPI* 75.75): 'Turlough Lynagh has preyed him of 400 kine, 60 mares, 200 swine, 300 sheep, and killed 16 of his followers. License of revenge. Scots at Loughfoyle.'

31 Copy of letter in hand of S, Baron of Dungannon to Grey (*CSPI* 75.84): 'Turlough Lynagh's intention to invade the Pale. Grey to send forces immediately to defend the borders. Has 25 horsemen in pay and desires more.'

September

2 Copy of letter in hand of S, Sir Nicholas Bagenal to Grey, Newry (*CSPI* 76.1): 'Sends T. Lynagh's letter. The party for whose death he challengeth Magennis so hotly was a most notorious thief and murderer. Turlough with 5,000 men assuredly bent to mischief, and has vowed to have his urraghs.'

4 Copy of letter in hand of S, Mr John Barnes to Grey, writing from Disert, Queen's County (*CSPI* 76.10): 'The rebels besiege Maryborough with a great force and expect James Eustace this night. Is fain to send this poor beggar with his letter.'

5 Pelham complains to Lord Grey that a letter by the latter's secretary (possibly S) was not 'considerately written'.

6 Pelham and Sir Henry Wallop arrive in Dublin.

7 S probably present at Grey's investiture as Lord Deputy in St. Patrick's Cathedral, Dublin. Grey took the oath and received the Sword of State from Pelham.

9 S accompanies Grey and Pelham to Drogheda. Wallop writes to Walsingham: 'The vij[th] herof S[r]. William Pelham in his owne person delivered the sworde to my Lo: Deputie, moste willinge to be dischardged of it'.

11 Armada sights Dingle Bay. Some of the ships are dispersed. The remaining force heads for Smerwick.

12–13 Papal force of Italians and Spaniards lands at Smerwick.

20 S paid £29 15s for rewards to messengers.

30 S pays out £12 15s as rewards to messengers.

October

6 S accompanies Grey on military expedition to Dingle to engage with the papal forces ensconced in the fort of Dunanoir – The Golden Fort – at Smerwick.

17 S leaves Cork for Limerick with Grey and army.
27 English galleons enter Dingle Bay. The papal fort, made only of earth, suffers a barrage of artillery.
29 Future publication of *SC* assigned to John Harrison the younger.
31 S and English forces reach Smerwick.

November

7–8 S with Grey when the Lord Deputy attacks The Golden Fort at Smerwick.
8 Guiseppe and Petruccio Barducci, author of a subsequent account of the massacre, go this evening to see Grey. S and Captain Edward Denny are mentioned by Barducci as benefiting from the colonel as hostage. Barducci claims that S and others profited from the massacre through ransoms for hostages.
9 This morning, the besieged fort surrenders and some 600 Spanish and Italian troops are massacred.
12 Copy of letter in hand of S, Lord Grey to the Queen, Smerwick (*CSPI* 78.29): 'The three causes which greatly hindered his marching. The stormy and raging weather. Admiral Winter's arrival. John Zouche and Captain Mackworth. Good John Cheke's wound and ecstasy. Battery of the fort. Parley. John Zouche. Captain William Pears, trench-master, a very industrious man. Speech of the Spanish captain sent by J. Martines de Ricaldi, Governor of Bilbao. Grey's characteristic answer. The colonel, with 12 of his chief gentlemen, trailing their ensigns rolled up, present their lives and the fort. Nov. 9, 600 put to the sword, of whom 400 were gallant and goodly persons. Captain Byngham a great jewel. Commends the bearer. Expects more Spaniards. Will leave J. Zouche as colonel, with 400 footmen and 50 horse, for the defence of the coast. Finds the people hard and stiff-necked, far from loving obedience. Can hardly get any to overthrow the fort.' The letter itself (*SP* 78.29) describes the eleventh hour submission of the Spanish colonel thus: 'at my handes no condition of compositions were they to expecte, other then y^t simply they should render me ye forte, & yield theyre selves to my will for lyfe or death: w^t this answere he departed; after which there was one or two courses two and fro more, to have gotten a certeinty for some of their lief, but fynding that yt would not bee, ye Coronell

him self about Sunne setting came forth, & requested respite w^t surcease of armes till ye nexte morning, & then he would give a resolute answere; fynding y^t to bee but a gayne of tyme for them & losse of the same for my self, I definitely answered I would not graunt y^t, & therefore presently either y^t he tooke my offer or elles retourne & I would fall to my busines. He then embraced my knees, simply putting him self to my mercy, onely he prayed y^t for y^t might hee might abyde in ye Forte, and y^t in ye morning all should be put into my hands: I asked hostages for ye performance; they were given.'

27 Treasurer Wallop and Waterhouse write to Burghley: 'The gladsome news of the slaughter of the Spaniards will entertain the Court a day or two.'

28 Letter in hand of S, Grey to Burghley, Limerick, showing S to have been at Smerwick (*BM Add.* Ms 33924, f6. Reproduced by Jenkins [1937] pp. 338–9): 'And thus praying yo^{re} L. [Lordship] to hasten hither moer store of victual w^t speed, for this will last no tyme to speake of.' S leaves Limerick for Clonmel with Grey, who wishes to avert a rumoured rebellion in the English Pale.

30 S and Grey arrive in Clonmel. Letter in hand of S, Grey to Sir Francis Walsingham, Clonmel (*CSPI* 76.68): 'He cannot pleasure the bearer Mr Kirton with the charge of a band.'

December

12 S paid £43 19s 3d for rewards to messengers. S pays out to messengers the sum of £18 16s 10d. The Queen writes to Grey, perhaps conveying the court's initial reaction to Smerwick: 'The mighty hand of the Almightiest power hath showed manifest the force of His strength in the weakness of feeblest sex, and minds this year to make men ashamed ever hereafter to disdain us. In which action I joy that you have been chosen the instrument of His glory, which I mean to give you no cause to forethink. Your loving sovereign, Eliz. R.'

22 Letter in hand of S, Grey to the Queen (*CSPI* 79.24.I; reproduced in part by Plomer [1923] p. 205, fig. 3): 'His sorrow that such nobles should be touched with faithless hearts. Chancellor Gerrarde's great policy and intolerable travail to the peril of his life. Archbishop of Dublin's constancy in this service by avouching his charge against the Earl. Delvin's

obstinate affection to Popery. His obedience to her warning against being strict in religion is very harmful. Prey of 1,000 kine taken from the rebels. Askeaton attacked. Clanrycard to be threatened for his sons' rebellion. Lord Garratt's escape.'

23 Letter endorsed by S, Grey to Queen, from Dublin (*CSPI* 79.26): 'Committal of the Baron Delvin and the Earl of Kildare to Dublin Castle for aiding in the rebellion in the Pale. Secretary Fenton, the bearer, to be credited.' S probably present when Chancellor Gerrard openly accuses the Earl of Kildare and his son-in-law, Christopher Nugent, fourteenth Baron Delvin, of treason, at Grey's Council Table in Dublin. Grey detains Kildare and Delvin in Dublin Castle. Kildare was a patron of Richard Stanyhurst, the Dublin writer, and had been, like Desmond before him, an ally of the Leicester–Sidney Circle. With his arrest, Leicester's interest in Ireland was muted. Edward Waterhouse writes to Walsingham in the context of a growing climate of concern at court over the Smerwick massacre: 'If the Queen will use mildness with the traitors, she would do better to discharge her army at once.'

31 S paid £10 as half-year's salary as secretary to Lord Grey.

Publication of Spenser–Harvey correspondence by Henry Bynneman, in a two-part volume, London: 1. *Three proper, wittie, familiar Letters: lately passed betwene two Universitie men: touching the Earthquake in April last, and our English refourmed Versifying*, and 2. *Two other, very commendable Letters, of the same mens writing: both touching the foresaid Artificiall Versifying, and cerain other Particulars*. The second volume contains earlier letters. S's two letters are dated from Leicester House, 5 October 1579 (including a letter of 15–16 October) and from Westminster, 'Quarto Nonas Aprilis 1580' (2 April, possibly in error for 10 April). The correspondence mentions *FQ* and alludes to S's 'lost' works: *Dreames* (see under 1579), *Dying Pellicane* (most likely an allegory of the death of Christ), both referred to by S as 'fully finished', *Epithalamion Thamesis* ('whyche Booke I dare undertake wil be very profitable for the knowledge, and rare for the Invention, and manner of handling'; possibly revised in *FQ* IV xi), *Nine Comoedies*, named after the Nine Muses (praised by Harvey for 'the finenesse of plausible Elocution' and 'the rarenesse of Poetical Invention') and the Latin *Stemmata Dudleiana* – in praise of the Leicester lineage. The correspondence includes S's 'Iambicum Trimetrum' and two short fragments in which he applies quantitative classical metres to English versification.

Sometime between now and 1585, Abrahaum Fraunce composes *The Sheapheardes Logike: conteyning the praecepts of that art put downe by Ramus; examples fet owt of the Sheapheards Kalender*, with numerous quotations from *SC*, in BM Ms. Add. 34,361, ff. 3–28.

1581

January
S remains in Dublin.

February
c.15 S probably accompanies Grey on a military venture directed against the O'Connors of Connaught.

March
1   Letter endorsed by S, Grey to Walsingham, Dublin (*CSPI* 81.1): 'Sends the examinations of Burnel and another. Conference between the Archbishop of Dublin and the Earl of Kildare concerning James Eustace. Sir Henry Bagenall allegeth that the day after the assembly at Tara, the Archbishop revealed to him some part of the talk.'
2   Letter endorsed by S, Grey to Walsingham, Dublin (*CSPI* 81.4): 'Sends another examination. Prays that Meaghe may be apprehended. The plot of Baltinglas. Rumours raised against him for committing Kildare.'
7   Document in hand of S, Malby-Burke Articles, Togher, Mayo (*CSPI* 81.15): 'Articles between Sir N. Malbie and Richard Yn Yren Burke, alias McWilliam Eighter, whereby that title is confirmed to him and he promises to banish all Scots and rebels.'
11 Copy of Latin letter in hand of S, Miler Magrath to Sir Lucas Dillon, Toom, Tipperary (*CSPI* 81.20): 'McCarthy More, McCarthy Reagh, the O'Sullivans, &c., have joined the rebels. Likelihood that the Munster and Connaught rebels will unite and form one army with the rebels of Ulster, and a great number of Scots. Private message to the Archbishop that the rebels will set upon the English this summer.'
13 Copy of letter in hand of S, the earl of Ormond to Grey, Cork

(*CSPI* 81.36.I): 'Barry Roe having taken a prey of Ormond's horses, Ormond entered Carbery and warded his castles for the Queen. Sir Owen McCarthy and others brought to Cork. David Barry's complaint that Sir Warham Sentleger and Rawley had procured commissions for killing him and warding his father's castles. Sir John of Desmond and the Browns repulsed from preying Kilmallock. Thomas and Ulick Brown slain.'

14 Letter endorsed by S, Grey to Burghley, Dublin (*CSPI* 81.27): 'Uncertainty of the peace with Turlough Lynagh. More men. Victual'. Lodowick Bryskett, confirmed in office of controller of the customs on wines, immediately hands over to S the office of registrar or clerk of Faculties in the Irish Court of Chancery. The office is not sold by Bryskett but given to S 'free from the Seale in respect he ys Secretarie to the right honorable the Lord Deputie' (*Fiants.*, Eliz., no. 3694).

16 Copy of document certified by S (*CSPI* 81.36.II): 'Examinations of Christopher Lumbard Fitz Jasper of Waterford, Robert Strange, and William Lincoll Fitz Andrew, showing the current report in Spain of the garrison at Smerwick.'

20 Document in hand of S, Burke's submission to Malby (*CSPI* 81.39): 'Submission of Richard In Yren Burke, alias McWilliam, to Sir N. Malbie. He confesses his rebellion and prays to be confirmed in the name and lordship of McWilliam Eighter.'

22 S appointed as registrar or clerk of Faculties in the Irish Court of Chancery, an office he holds for seven years: Edmund Spenser 'gent., secretary of the deputy' granted the office of 'registrar or clerk in Chancery, for faculties under the statute 28 Hen. VIII, to hold during good behaviour, with the fees belonging to the office' (*Fiants*, Eliz. no. 3694). That S had a deputy for this office until September 1582, while he was serving as Grey's private secretary, is suggested by the following: 'Edmunde Spencer, Register or Clerke in the Chauncerie of the faculties within the kingdome of Ireland . . . a depu[ty] all[owed], canc. 22 die Marcii 23 Eliz.' (*Harleian* MS 4107). The Act of Faculties, levelled against the 'intollerable exaction of great sums of money by the Bishop of Rome', provided for the appointment of 'one sufficient Clerk, being learned in the course of the Chancery, which shall always be attendant on the Lord Chancellor or the Lord Keeper of the Great Seal, and shall make, write and enroll the confirmations

of all such licenses, dispensations, instruments and other writings as shall be brought under the Archbishop's seal, there to be confirmed or enrolled, taking for his pains such reasonable sums of money as hereafter, by this Act, shall be limited for the same'.

23 Letter endorsed by S, Grey to Leicester (*CSPI* 81.42): 'Discourse of Sir Nicholas Malbie touching his late journey against Richard In Yren Burke, now McWilliam Eighter, and the Scots that he had hired. One of Grey's sons has this morning died.'

28 S paid £52 4s 10d as rewards for messengers. S pays out £39 3s 8d as rewards to messengers.

April

6 Letter thought to be endorsed by S, Grey to Walsingham, Dublin (*CSPI* 82.6): 'The need of a Parliament for trial of the prisoners. The calling of new Lords. Stephen Kerroan, Bishop of Kilmacduagh, to be Bishop of Clonfert in the country of Clanricard. Sir William Stanley and Capt. Russell have burnt Feagh McHugh's house of Ballinacor. Captain Mackworth has put 100 of the best of the O'Mores to the sword. Grey must have more money or be recalled.' Letter endorsed by S, Grey to Burghley, Dublin (*Cecil Papers* 11.91, no. 970): 'Thanks him for his letter by Mr. Fent, and will ever cherish his good will. Marvels at Ned Denny's report. Is much contented that Burghley is satisfied with his assertion in a matter that none of Denny's instructions touched. Thanks Burghley for his care about the victuals, and wishes the under officers were as careful in executing as he in directing. None of the victuals lately sent have arrived; prays for honest officers to issue them when they do come. "The little service in Munster I cannot altogether excuse; and yet, my Lord, there hath been more done than I perceive is conceived. For my part, without it be of some importance, I take no delight to advertise of every common person's head that is taken off; otherwise, I could have certified of a hundred or two of their lives ended since my coming from these parts, but indeed some hindrance it brought to the greater service that the garrisons would not remain in some of the places appointed first of, by reason that their victuals could not be as readily conveyed to them as was hoped of". The imperfections of the bands due to the evil

choice of the men sent, and to a pestilent ague prevalent
during the whole winter. Hopes it will soon cease, and that the
fresh men to be sent will be maintained in a better state.
Agrees that the peril of Ireland lies most in foreign aids,
chiefly in the north. The disquiet and mischief of the land will
grow daily more and more, unless speedily looked into and
prevented, as he has often certified. "To force the rebel from
the seaside we need not, for the inward country is his own
seeking, finding there all his relief and sustenance, and all our
travel is to drive him to the coasts, where neither fastness for
himself, nor succour for his create [sic], but seldom is found".
Removal of the garrison of the Dingle Castle Magha, where
the rebel Earl of Desmond hath walked most of the winter.
The said garrison so visited with the sickness that not forty
able bodies were left in it. Hopes ere the summer goes that the
enemy will be otherwise "layed unto". Has heard nothing
touching the removal of Collman. Doubts not his Lordship is
acquainted by his late advertisements with the good estate of
Connaught, through Sir Nicholas Malby's services. The
occasion of sending the bearer, Justice Dillon, is that further
instructions may be received regarding the trial of the meaner
prisoners, there being objections to the ordinary course of
proceedings. Desires all credit for the bearer. The infiniteness
of his toil prevents him from writing as often as he would.'
Endorsed '6 April 1581. The Lord Deputie of Ireland to my
lord by Mr Dillon.'

7 Letter thought to be endorsed by S, Grey to Walsingham (*CSPI*
   82.16): 'As to the delivery of his letter to the Privy Council'.

22 Letter endorsed by S, Grey to Burghley, Dublin (*Cecil Papers*
   11.94, no. 976): 'Fresh advertisements from the north confirm
   the rebellious attempts of Tyrlogh. Finding his [i.e. Grey's]
   demands for the preventing thereof not met, he could not but
   despatch a messenger of purpose, with letters to the Queen,
   and also to the Council, soliciting a "soon despatch".
   Burghley's furtherance is a special hope with him. Prays the
   matter may be well weighed and answered, or else that he
   may be removed. Has set down the whole matter at some
   length in his letter to the Council, so need not repeat it.
   Thanks Burghley for the victuals, whereof a great part has
   arrived, and the rest is hourly expected. Begs that some
   money may be sent, or it will go hard with them.' [Postscript]

'Understands that some go about to get estates in certain things about him. Begs that, by Burghley's continued favour, the caveat may be renewed. A servant of his shall bring a note of the parcels'.

26 Letter in hand of S, Grey to the Queen, Dublin (*CSPI* 82.54): 'More force. A most dishonourable composition with Turlough at his own will and during his own pleasure. The taking of kerne and churls every day. Murders, stealths, rapes, and all other insolencies to have free allowance, or the perpetrator will become a traitor to defend his cause. Elizabeth's great fear, due reverence, and sound knowledge of God. General pardon disapproved of. Grey offered Desmond himself pardon against his instruction. Grey has never taken the life of any, however evil, that submitted.'

29 Copy of letter in hand of S, Ormond and Commissioners to Grey, from Cork (*CSPI* 83.6.I): 'Countess of Desmond. Her sister has a protection to withdraw with two or three of her servants to her brother the baron of Dunboyne.' Copy of document certified by S (*CSPI* 83.6.II): 'Petition of the Countess of Desmond to the Lord General and Council of Munster, for license to go to England with her daughters.'

May

6 S appears 'in propria persona' in the Court of Exchequer, Dublin (*Memoranda Roll*, 21st–24th Eliz., membrane 108).

10 Letter endorsed by S, Grey and Council to the Lord General and Council of Munster, Dublin (*CSPI* 83.6.III): 'Disapprove of the arrogant petition of the Countess of Desmond, who wilfully fell from her protection and furthered the treason of bringing in strangers.'

12 Letter endorsed by S, Grey to Walsingham (*CSPI* 83.6): 'The ill state of Munster will shortly show itself. No help so long as Ormond is here, although Leycestre and Walsingham will not believe it. Barry Roe, who killed George Champern, is protected, and David Barry is proclaimed. Turlough Lynagh has preyed Knockfergus. Doctor Chapman to be Dean of St. Patrick's. The composition for cess ends May 31, and must not be renewed. The bearer Roger Radford to have commission to collect such Irish writings as were with his late master, Chancellor Gerrarde, at his death.'

Towards the end of this month S accompanies Grey on a mission to pacify the O'Tooles, O'Byrnes and Kavanaghs of Wicklow and Wexford.

June

9   Letter addressed by S, Grey to Walsingham, Wexford (*CSPI* 83.43): 'Desires to be recalled. Has signified to Ormond Her Majesty's pleasure for his discharge. Turlough Lynagh.'

10   Letter addressed by S, Grey to Privy Council, Wexford (*CSPI* 83.45): 'His journey against the Kavanaghs. Repairs Castle Kevan and Castle Comin. Loss of some of his plate in a pass. Harrington's charge. Takes a prey from Crephin McMurrough Kavanagh and burns McVadock's country. Walter Gallte Kavanagh, who has committed so many murders this last 20 years, executed. Discharge of the bands of Cecil and Hoorde. The sacrifice of the good subject by the general pardon. Turlough Lynagh. Ormond contentedly submitteth himself to the Queen's pleasure for the ceasing of his authority in Munster. 300 Scots drawn from O'Rourke by Malbie and employed by Grey.' Letter in secretary hand of S, Grey to Walsingham, Wexford (*CSPI* 83.47): 'in behalf of the bearer, who has served under Capt. Cecil'. S pays out £47 2*s* 8*d* as rewards to messengers.

24   S paid £15 for 'paper, yncke, and parchment' for year ending this day.

26   S paid £10 as half year's salary as secretary.

July

5   Letter addressed by S from Dublin, Grey to Walsingham (*CSPI* 84.3): 'His journey upon the Pale rebels. The message he received by Ned. Denny from Her Majesty's self. Her dislike of the service. The service he has done sufficient to grace the Minister and declare the good favour of God. Intreats his recall. Captain Hoorde's band wasted with sickness and cassed at his own request.'

10   Letter addressed by S from Dublin, Grey to Privy Council (*CSPI* 84.12): 'Creon McCaier Kavanagh repaired to his camp at Simolins and was received to grace. Murrough Oge Kavanagh has put in pledges to Captain George Carew at Leighlin for all the Kavanaghs of Idrone. Trial of Nicholas Deverox. Richard Butler, Ferdorogh Pursell, and his brother,

very infamous for their ill-doings, condemned. Captain Macworth's service upon the sept of Art Boy. The freeholders of the Kinsheloughe put in pledges. Maisterson and Sinnot. The Glins hunted. Francis Stafford's service in Shileloughe. Garrisons planted to subdue Feagh McHugh. Desmond's force of 1,000 attacked by Zouche, and the Chanter of Limerick, being a tall horseman, who came out of Spain with James Fitz Maurice, was slain by the Colonel's hand. Disposition of the bands in Munster on the discharge of Ormond. Turlough Lynagh has vowed to stir in Ireland if any attempt be made by Scotland against England. The Bishop of Waterford acquitted of the slander raised upon him.' Letter in hand of S, Grey to the Privy Council, Dublin (*CSPI* 84.13): 'Certain of O'Donnell's chief captains and many of his men slain by Turlough Lynagh, who is burning and slaying in Tirconnell.' Letter in hand of S, Grey to Walsingham, Dublin (*CSPI* 84.14; reproduced by Plomer [1923] figs 1 and 2): 'The bickering between Turlough Lynagh and O'Donnell. Urgent want of money.' This letter also bears an interesting endorsement by S, followed by his signature: 'For her Ma^{ts} sp[ec]iall affaires. To the honorable my esp[ec]iall good frend Sr Franc[e]s Walsingham, knight, Chief Secretarie to her Matie. Hast hast post haste for lyfe. D[ate]d at Dublin the xth of Julie. Ed Sp[en]ser.'

15   S secures lease under commission of the castle and manor of Enniscorthy, County Wexford.

18   Letter in hand of S, Grey to Walsingham, Dublin (*CSPI* 84.28): 'to further the suit of his servant, Richard Mompesson, touching his Spanish prisoner, who has escaped with the privity of his keeper'.

Toward the end of this month and the early part of the next, S accompanies Grey on his northern sojourn.

August

2   S probably attended Grey while he negotiated with Turlogh Lynagh O'Neill at the Blackwater. Lodowick Bryskett is one of the commissioners sent over the Blackwater to settle final terms with O'Neill.

10   Letter in hand of S, Grey to the Queen, Dublin (*CSPI* 85.5): 'His stay two or three days at the Blackwater for Turlough

Lynagh, lacking beef and grass. He sends his wife with his griefs for injuries done him by Dungannon. His flat refusal to the Knight Marshal to deliver up William Nugent. Deputy's parley with Turlough. Commissioners sent over the Blackwater. O'Donnell oppressed because he would not retain Scots. Zouche has again done good service upon the rebels.' Letter thought to be addressed by S, Grey to Queen, Dublin (*CSPI* 85.6): 'His intended journey to the mountains against Baltinglas. George Carew to surrender his possessions in exchange. The Kavanaghs to have a Governor set over them.'

12 Letter addressed by S, Grey to Privy Council, Dublin (*CSPI* 85.13): 'His journey and peace with Turlough Lynagh, who put off his hat and joyed that he had peace. The intolerable pride and insolency of Turlough Lynagh. The good acceptation of Zouche's service. Fidelity of O'Donnell's followers. Sentleger's appointment as colonel, with the dislike of Ormond. O'Rourke's spoil in the Annaly. Execution of rebels at Arklow by Sir W. Stanley. Captain Deering has slain 14 near Powerscourt.'

c.15 S accompanies Grey on expedition against the Leinster rebels, led by Baltinglas and Feagh McHugh.

26 Letter addressed by S, Grey to Burghley, Dublin (*Cecil Papers* 11.113, no. 1026): 'Finds the whole store at Cork utterly spent, and the garrison thereby in no small penury. Prays for speedy supply, and that the ships bringing the proportion for those parts be directed henceforth to Youghal and not to Cork, the staple there fitting far better the garrison's turn. Through the great defaultments & allowances of old dues, scarce 3,000l. of the last treasure allotted will come unto them, whereof necessary payments of corn and beeves being made, not 2,000l. will rest for the officers, soldiers, and himself. What that sum will do amongst so many, & where so much is due, he leaves to Burghley's consideration. Begs that suits upon private affection and favour may not be allowed to hinder the service there. The great need of money: "without ready coin, I put not one bit of meat in my mouth, nor feed my horses". The "not overhastiness" of Her Majesty to afford the supply. Knows not what in the world they shall do without it. That now to be received is "none other than as good never a whit, as never the better". Expects to write again ere two days be ended.'

28 Grey writes to Walsingham (*CSPI* 85.27), advocating a divide and conquer strategy for the defeat of the rebels.

30 Letter addressed by S, Grey to Burghley, Dublin (*Cecil Papers* 11.114, no. 1029), 'Articles that Feaghe McHughe is bound to accomplish upon his coming in': 'This pacification with the Obirns, Feagh Mack Heughe, and Connor MacCormack . . . is a course not the surest for the State, because the Irish are so addicted to Treachery and Breach of Fidelity, as longer then they find the Yoke in their Neck, they respect not either Pledge, Affinity, or Duty . . . considering as well the Unsteadiness of the Irish of these Parts (whom no Pledges do sufficiently tye) as specially the Looseness of Tirlough Lennoughe, whose Word only, or Oath, is all the Band and Assurance I have upon him for this late Peace; which Oath is in his religion to be dispensed withall by any of his Romish priests, as soon as he spieth an opportunity to break for advantage.'

September

11 Letter addressed by S, Grey to Walsingham, Dublin (*CSPI* 85.36): 'Sufficiency of the bearer Sir W. Stanley'.

12 Letter addressed by S, Grey to Privy Council, Dublin (*CSPI* 85.37): 'Commends the bearer Mr. Parker for the manful defence of the castle of Askeaton against the frequent attempts of the rebels.'

c.15 S leaves Dublin with Grey to confront the Munster rebels, journeying by way of Kilkenny, Waterford, Dungarvon, Lismore, Youghal and Cork.

October

19 Entry of payment to Colonel John Zowche, per bill due to S for £32 (*SPI* 97.17.I, not calendered): 'A note of all suche monye as hath been paid and imprested by Sir Henry Wallopp Knight Treasurer at Warres in Ireland to sundrye Captaines serving in the said province [Munster] betwene the fyrst September 1579 and the laste of August 1582, as hereafter uppon everye captains head particularlye as sett down appereth, viz. John Zowche esquier, Collonell in Munster, xix[th] October 1581, per bill due to Edmond Spencer xxxijli.'

November

6   Letter in hand of S, Grey to the Queen, Dublin (*CSPI* 86.50): 'The diversely misgathered memorials of Oct. 11, shall be answered before long. Generality of revolt at his entrance into the government. The great mischief by the proclamation of pardon. Two Englands unable for such a continual charge. The only peace at this time to be effected is by surrender of the whole realm to the rebels. Prayer to be recalled.' Letter addressed by S, Grey to the Privy council, Dublin (*CSPI* 86.51): 'Necessity for his journey into Munster by the departure of Sir Warham Sentleger. Death of the late Baron of Upper Ossory. Final end between the Earl of Ormond, the Viscount Mountgarret, and the now Baron of Upper Ossory. Pardon to James Meaghe, now called James McKedaughe O'More. March through Waterford, Dungarvan, Lismore, Youghal and Cork. Of 500 pardoned, not 60 appeared. Captain Apsley's band in Carbery. Manner of placing Zouche as Chief Colonel of Munster, with a plot for the prosecution of the war. Lord Roche, Sir Cormac McTeige, Sir Donough McCarthy, Sir Thomas of Desmon, and Maurice Roche. 60 of the townsmen of Cashel slain by the traitors. John Shreif acquitted of the escape of Patrick Fitzmaurice. Most of the English families in the Pale touched with the late conspiracy'. Letter addressed by S, Grey to Walsingham, Dublin (*CSPI* 86.53): 'Has desired the Earl of Leycestre to show Walsingham the answers now sent to the chief parts in the memorial. The trial of the Pale conspirators. His bodily health will not suffer him to continue Deputy. Walsyngham to obtain for him his writings and warrants according to promise. Walsyngham's travail to match Grey's niece. His desire to be at the marriage.'

9   S pays out £42 19s 2d as rewards to messengers.

28 Letter in hand of S, Grey to Burghley, Dublin (*Cecil Papers* 12.16, no. 1078): 'Recommending the bearer, Sir Nicholas Malby, for his services in Ireland. Asks that Anthony Lawe's pension may be continued and paid in England.'

December

6   S receives the official lease for the Abbey and Manor of Enniscorthy, together with the site of a Franciscan monastery, Co. Wexford, the property described as 'the house of Friars of

Enniscortie, the Manor of Enniscortie, and a ruinous castle and weir there'.

9　Conveyance of Enniscorthy by S to Richard Synnot of Ballybrenan, Co. Wexford. Synnot, who had served as sheriff of Wexford, was in fact a previous owner of Enniscorthy, having been granted it in 1575 (*Fiants*, Eliz. no. 2663). Synnot later leased part of this property to Undertreasurer Wallop (see entry for 6 January 1586). A MS book in the Exchequer Records Office in Dublin giving an account of the Revenues of the Queen's lands and possessions, compiled by Nicholas Kenney as deputy of the Auditor-General, contains the following entry of a receipt: 'From Sir Henry Wallop, Knt. (assignee of Richard Synnott, gent., assignee of Edmund Spencer, gent.) now farmer of all the lands of the late manor of Enniscorthie; per annum, £11 13s. 4d.' It has been suggested that with the money from this conveyance S leases the dissolved Augustinian friary at New Ross, Co. Wexford from Edmund Butler, second Viscount Mountgarret, of Ballyragget, Kilkenny, who served several times as a commissioner of musters for Co. Wexford. S later sells this property to Sir Anthony Colclough. Since Colclough died in 1584, the conveyance of New Ross must have occurred by that year. The property was passed on to his son, Sir Thomas Colclough.

10　Letter in hand of S, Grey to Burghley, Dublin (*Cecil Papers* 12.19, no. 1081): 'Being ready to send away his former letters, he received Burghley's of 25 September, whereunto, by reason of their oldness, he replies at once. Concerning the dislikes as are conceived of the charges of this realm, trusts that in the general answer to the memorial full satisfaction is yielded. Thanks Burghley for his promise not to suffer any defalcations upon bills there to be made; but being informed that, out of the present mass which is now to come over, only £5,000 is appointed to the growing charges of this realm he cannot but think a very strait hand therein held, considering the need wherewith the garrison is pinched, whom how to relieve he sees not, unless it be thought that men may feed of air.' Letter addressed by S, Grey and Council to the Privy Council, Dublin (*CSPI* 87.32): 'Special commendation of the 16 years service of the bearer Capt. Geo. Thornton. Smerwick, Carrickfoyle, Askeaton, and Dingle Cush.'

29　Letter in hand of S, Grey to Walsingham, Dublin (*CSPI* 87.64):

'They cannot exactly follow the late direction for issue of the treasure, considering the exigence of their distress.'

Publication of John Derricke's *The Image of Irelande*, London. Having been assigned to John Harrison the younger, the second edition of *SC* is published by Thomas East. The Cambridge comedy *Pedantius* is staged in Trinity College. Script published in 1631. Pedantius and his pupil, Leonidas, thought to stand for Harvey and Spenser. Philip Sidney composes his treatise on poetry, published in 1595 as *The Defence of Poesie* and as *An apologie for Poetrie*. Sidney refers to S thus: 'The Sheepheards Kellender, hath much *Poetrie* in his Egloges, indeed woorthie the reading, if I be not deceived. That same framing of his style to an old rusticke language, I dare not allow: Since neither *Theocritus* in Greeke, *Virgil* in Latine, nor *Sanazara* in Italian, did affect it.'

1582

Sometime in the spring of this year, at a gathering of friends in Bryskett's cottage a mile and a half from Dublin, S asks to be excused from a disquisition on moral philosophy on the grounds that he has already undertaken such a task in *FQ*. This (fictional?) exchange is recorded in Bryskett's *Discourse of Civill Life* (1606). Among those present are Sir Robert Dillon, M. Dormer, Thomas Smith (apothecary), Thomas Digges, Warham St. Leger, Nicholas Dawtrey, John Long, Thomas Norris and Christopher Carleill.

January
3 Letter in hand of S, Grey to the Privy Council, Dublin (*CSPI* 88.2): 'His necessity in applying 3,000l. out of the 15,000l. to other uses than paying the discharged bands. Their Lordships to move her Majesty to choose some other to wield so great a burden and cross'.
7 Letter addressed by S, Grey to Walsingham, Dublin (*CSPI* 88.9): 'The discharge of pensioners. Payment of merchants' and captains' bills. The impossibility of following the directions from Her Majesty. Has not received the packet commanding the discharge of all but 3,000. Pypho's wrong information. Has of late found very suspicious dealing amongst all his best esteemed associates. Dislikes not to be

informed of the charges against him. Sir N. Malbie to be despatched. Brian Fytzwylliams's lieutenant and company discharged [partly in cipher].'

12   Letter in hand of S, Grey to Burghley, Dublin (*CSPI* 88.12): 'The impracticable plot for Munster delivered by Capt. Rawley [Walter Raleigh]. The garrison of Munster almost utterly starved by Bland. Subsidy. The arch rebel Sir John slain. James Fitz John of Strangalie, a notorious knave.'

13   S in Dublin when head of Sir John Desmond was delivered to Grey by Colonel Zouche. It was publicly displayed like that of Pollente in *FQ* V ii 19. Letter addressed by S, Grey to Walsingham, Dublin (*CSPI* 88.15): 'The empacketed letter to the Council to be answered with speed. John of Desmond's head brought as a new year's gift from the Colonel. Her Majesty might do well to bestow on him the traitor's lands. The proclamation gives 500l. for his killing, but where is the money?'

25   Letter in hand of S, Grey to the Queen, Dublin (*CSPI* 88.39): 'Grey to Queen. He received her letter for discharge of soldiers dated 12 Dec. but this day. The manner of his bestowing the rebels' land falsely reported to Her Majesty. He craves to be heard before condemnation, and to be recalled.'

27   Letter addressed by S, Grey to Walsingham, Dublin (*CSPI* 88.40): 'The reduction of the garrison to 3,000. His grief at the faults found with his dealings. His associates take pleasure at the news of Her Majesty's offence. Burghley's sharp letter terming this place a gulf of consuming treasure. Ed. Denny discharged. Walsyngham to help him to the Abbey of Fowre in Westmeath. J. Dyve. W. Sentleger. Baron of Dungannon's good service in taking the principal practiser in the last conspiracy, John Cusake. J. Cusake utterly confounds the Lord and Lady of Delvin. Sir Lucas Dillon, Sir Robert Dillon, and Sir John Plunket to have some reward besides words. If John Cusake say truth there will not one honest Nugent be found here. The further discharge. Prays to be called home.' On the same day, Grey writes again to Walsingham: 'Lord Deputy Grey to Walsyngham. Note of the lands and goods of the rebels given by the Lord Deputy since his coming into Ireland. Amongst other things a lease to Sir William Russell; Monkton to Sir Henry Wallop; . . . Galmoreston to Capt. Ed. Denny; Ralwagh to Thomas Lee; . . . Barry's Island to Captain Walter

Rawley; . . . a farm to Rice ap Hugh, the Provost Marshall; the
goods of Browne of Dunboyne to William Piers, late lieutenant
to Captain William Piers, Junior, maimed in service; the lease
of a house in Dublin belonging to Baltinglas for six years to
come unto Edmund Spenser, one of the Lord Deputy's
secretaries, valued at 5l; . . . of goods of Teige Oge O'Ferrall to
Lawrence Taaffe, servant to Sir Lucas Dillon, for service done
upon O'Rourke; of a custodiam of John Eustace's land of the
Newland to Edmund Spenser, one of the Lord Deputy's
secretaries.' S to pay annual rent of £3.

February
  4 Letter addressed by S, Grey and Council to Privy Council,
     Dublin (*CSPI* 89.11): 'The reasons he defers the cassing of the
     700 till the last of February.'
  5 Copy of document in hand of S, John Nugent's Confession,
     Dublin (*CSPI* 89.18; first page reproduced by Plomer [1923]
     fig. 4): 'John Nugent's confession, being a plain discourse of
     William Nugent's rebellious acts. The search made for his
     youngest son Christopher. The behaviour of his wife Gennett
     Marwards, wherein Ellen Plunkett, wife to Nicholas Nugent,
     is touched'.
 10 The 'Book of Concordatums' gives details of 'suche Concordat
     as is alreadie paid by Sr. Henry Wallopp, knight Treasurer at
     warres there' to 'Edmond Spencer for rewards to messengers'.
     A further sum was paid out on this date. These messengers
     would be bearers of official dispatches and S would be acting
     as paymaster in his capacity as secretary to the Lord Deputy.
 13 Letter in hand of S, Grey to the Privy Council, Dublin (*CSPI*
     89.30): 'Commends the renewing of Her Majesty's good
     meaning to Neil McGeoghegan, the son of Rosse, who was
     wickedly murdered by Bryan. His dutiful mind towards Her
     Majesty.'
 18 Letter in hand of S, Grey to the Privy Council, Dublin (*CSPI*
     89.35): 'for payment to Clonmel of money owing to them by
     Captains Tanner, George Lower, and Thomas Morgan'.
  ? Undated letter, addressed by S, Grey to Walsingham (*CSPI*
     89.55): 'to obtain the remain of the pay due to Captain Acres'.

March
  1 Letter in hand of S, Grey to Walsingham, Dublin (*CSPI* 90.1):

'Report from Anthony Brabazon, Deputy Governor of Connaught, that the discharged soldiers were like to do some mischief. Robert Colom licensed to take 200 or 300 of them to the Low Countries. Walsyngham to write favourably in their behalf to Mr. John Norreys.'

14 Patent to Roland Cowyk as Clerk of Chancery for Faculties: 'That he shall have and enjoy the same severall offices in that our realme of Ireland [as he has in England], and be our Clerk of our Chancery there for the Faculties, and our sole Register for all manner of Appeales Ecclesiastical . . . in as ample manner as either our officers do use and exercise those severall offices here in England . . . and also the office of our Register of our late and new created Prerogative Court Ecclesiastical in Ireland' (*Liber Munerum Publicorum Hiberniae*, II, p. 29). Cowyk may have succeeded S. Alternatively, he could have acted as his deputy. The duties entailed writing and registering special ecclesiastical licences called 'faculties'.

23 Document in hand of S, 'Newes out of Munster', reporting the slaughter of Captain James Fenton's company (*BM Cotton Ms. Titus* B.XIII, f. 364. Reproduced by Jenkins [1935] p. 126): 'A note of certain Adv^ertizem^ts sent out of Mounster from Justice Meagh sr. (?) 23° Mart. Capt fenton coming by sea to help his men, whom he heard to bee distressed by the enemy, was in the way intercepted, all his men slayne, him self taken, or killed. Also the Rebells have layd siege to ye Castle of Bentrey, There is lately come out of Spayne unto the Rebells one Henry Mobryen a Priest. The same hath like wise bene adv^ertized by Tho. Burgate & others, that there is a Bishop come from ye Pope to Arlogh, appointed for Corke and Cloyne and y^t he giveth forth that an Army of iiij^C Saile is to come from Spayne into this Realme this Sommer.' James Fenton, Constable of Bearehaven and Commander of West Cork, was the brother of Geoffrey Fenton, the translator who went to Ireland with Spenser and became Secretary there.

24 Copy of letter in hand of S, Sir Edward Butler to Waterhouse (*CSPI* 90.31): 'His life sought. His brother the Earl's unkindness, who has taken from him his inheritance and purchased land. Injuries he receives of the Archbishop and Kennedies. His brother left no order for his security. Prays the Lord Deputy's protection and two months to remove from the town he is in.'

27 Letter in hand of S, Grey to the Privy Council, Dublin (*CSPI* 90.48): 'Recommends the humble request of Murrough Ne Doe O'Flaherty to surrender his lands and take them again of Her Majesty. The bearer his agent.'

28 Letter in hand of S, Grey and Council to Privy Council, Dublin (*CSPI* 90.52): 'Commend the bearer John Thirst, late ensign to Captain Dowdall, having many years discharged the parts of a tall soldier, and now lame and quite unprovided.'

April

4 S present at the trial of Chief Justice Nicholas Nugent at Trim, charged with complicity in the revolt of his uncle, William Nugent. Letter in hand of S, Grey to Walsingham, Trim (*CSPI* 91.11): 'Commends the bearer Patrick Barnewall'.

6 S witnesses execution of Nicholas Nugent.

8 Letter thought to be addressed by S, Grey to Walsingham, Dublin (*CSPI* 91.17): 'Trial and execution of Nicholas Nugent, late Justice of the Common Pleas. Edward Cusake, of Lismullin, condemned but saved. To inform the Queen of Grey's inability to hold the government any longer. His due allowance to be warranted, the treasurer refusing him payment.'

12 S paid once again 'for rewards to messengers'. Letter thought to be addressed by S, Grey to Privy Council, Dublin (*CSPI* 91.22): 'The trial, confession, and pardon of Edward Cusack. The trial, obstinacy, and execution of Nicholas Nugent late Chief Justice of the Common Pleas'. Document in hand of S, (*CSPI* 91.26; reproduced by Plomer [1923] fig. 5): 'A note of L[ett]res *and* copies sent to Mr. Secret. Walsingham xii Apr. [1582]', amongst which are the Pope's and Desmond's to O'Donnell.

19 Letter in hand of S, Grey and Council to Privy Council, Dublin (*CSPI* 91.38): 'Commend the bearer, wife to George Fitzgerald slain in a skirmish with the late mountain rebel.'

20 Sir Warham Sentleger informs Burghley that there are some sixty to seventy deaths every day due to plague and famine in Cork, 'which is but one street not half a quarter of a mile in length' (*CSPI* 91.41).

30 Letter in hand of S, Grey to Burghley, Dublin (*CSPI* 91.52): 'The 20 years tall service of the bearer James Vaughan, now discharged. His loss of limbs and of 1,000l by Turlough

Lynagh.' Letter in hand of S, Grey to Walsingham, Dublin (*CSPI* 91.53): 'Long service of Vaughan, late lieutenant to Jenkins. Favour to the causes he means to solicit.' Sentleger writes to Burghley informing him that over 30,000 people had perished over a six-month period during the Munster famine (*CSPI* 92.103).

May

7 Letter in hand of S, Grey to the Privy Council, Dublin (*CSPI* 92.9): 'Has received the depositions touching James Fitz Edmonds taken at Chester. Will proceed to examine him when he cometh.' Letter in hand of S, Grey to Walsingham, Dublin (*CSPI* 92.10): 'Justification of Captain Mackworth and Captain Cosby. Slender furtherance of service in rebuking men for venturing their lives and taking away rebels and villainous persons. Mr Henry Guildford's custodiam near Limerick. Grey likes not Captain Rawley's carriage or company. He has nothing to expect from him. Bowen restored to the office of serjeant-at-arms in Munster.'

9 Copy of letter in hand of S, Grey and Council to the Queen, Dublin (*CSPI* 92.11.I. Original calendered as *CSPI* 92.20): 'Answer to Her Majesty's letter of April 25. Manner of pursuing the concordatums. The custodiams granted to Dillon, Norreys, Byrne, and Bryskett. These custodiams are no hindrance to her revenues. The manner of the cess of the Pale. The butcherly massacre of the garrisons in Munster.' The 'Book of Concordatums' has this entry (*CSPI* 92.20.I):

Edmond Spencer for Rewards by him payd to messengers at sundrie times viz.:

ultimo Septembris	1580	by concordatum £	12.15.
xij Decembris	1580	"	18.16.10
xxviij March	1581	"	39. 3. 8
x June	1581	"	47. 2. 8
ix Nov^r	1581	"	42.19. 2
		In all £	160.17. 4.

This is a sub-total. The total sum paid to S as rewards for messengers during Grey's deputyship was £430 10s 2d.

10 Letter endorsed by S, Grey and Council to Queen, Dublin

(*CSPI* 92.25): 'In answer to the complaint laid against the Lord Deputy by Patrick Birmyngham. Particulars of his conduct, imprisonment, and release. Mr Garland dismissed.' Letter addressed by S, Grey to Walsingham, Dublin (*CSPI* 92.26): 'His answer to a malicious complaint. He hopes his time will be short, but will ever wish well to the State.'

11 Letter in hand of S, Grey and Council to Privy Council, Dublin (*CSPI* 92.30): 'In favour of the bearer, James Vaughan, late lieutenant to Captain Jenkins.'

15 Captain Humphrey Macworth, one of Grey's most ruthless officers, and a principal actor in the Smerwick massacre, is captured, tortured and killed by the O'Connors of Offaly.

16 Letter in hand of S, Grey to Walsingham, Dublin (*CSPI* 92.46): 'For a speedy answer to his letters touching a revenge of the O'Conors.'

22 Letter addressed by S, Grey to Walsingham, Dublin (*CSPI* 92.52): 'Arrival of Sir Nicholas Malbie May 21. The answer to the instructions and memorials. Kildare and Delvin are sent over. His revocation. His answers to the informations of Patrick Birmingham and the rest. Sends the draft of a warrant for his entertainment agreed on by the Treasurer and Auditor.'

25 Sir Nicholas White, Irish-born barrister and Master of the Rolls in Ireland, writes to Burghley: 'Her Majesty's clement and merciful disposition towards her people is the greatest comfort that ever came into this land, Elizabeth, the Amor Hiberniae above all the Princes that ever reigned.'

28 Letter in hand of S, Grey to the Privy Council, Dublin (*CSPI* 92.85): 'For favour to the requests of the bearer a discharged captain.' Letter addressed by S, Grey to Privy Council, Dublin (*CSPI* 92.86): 'The bearer Richard Marsh, late a horseman under the heading of Sir Edward Moore, to be considered in recompense of his hurt and disability.' S presumably accompanied Grey to revenge the death of Macworth.

By the end of this month famine and the plague had wiped out 90 per cent of the male population of Cork.

June
7 S probably with Grey at Phillipstown.
16 S probably with Grey at Monastervan.
21 Letter addressed by S, Grey to Walsingham, Dublin (*CSPI*

93.34): 'Of the difficulty as to Clanrycard, who by the memorial is expected to reclaim or suppress his wicked children. To procure Grey's repair to England. To afford his servant credit.'

22　Letter in hand of S, Grey to Burghley, Dublin (*CSPI* 93.46): 'The bearer, Beverley, repaireth to acquaint his Lordship with the imperfect state of the victualling before he will enter into the discharge of that office.'

24　S paid once more 'for rewards to messengers'.

29　Letter in hand of S, Grey to Walsingham, Dublin (*CSPI* 93.64): 'Sends two letters coming from England. Thomas Meagh to be examined on one of them. His repair over. Distrust of the Munster garrisons.' Copy of document certified by S, letter of Thomas Meagh to his brother James Meagh alias McKedagh O'More, dated May 17 (*CSPI* 93.64.I): 'To procure him money of Walter Ashpoll and others. The Earl of Kildare's hard dealings with him. Promises him preferment amongst the O'Mores. Warns him against Harpoll and Mackworth.'

Richard Stanyhurst's translation of the first four books of Virgil's *Aeneis*, dedicated to Patrick Plunket, Lord Baron of Dunsany, and influenced by the metrical theories of Gabriel Harvey, is published at Leyden.

July

10　Letter addressed by S, Grey and Council to Privy Council, Dublin (*CSPI* 94.15): 'Con O'Donnell with great force has spoiled and burnt the country under Malbie. No force can be sent to his aid. This outrage of T. Lynagh was not provoked by any discourtesy to the value of a hair. Sir Nicholas Malbie having been rebuked in England, will not lay any charge on Her Majesty or the country, which will be all wasted.'

15　S granted lease under commission for New Abbey, Kilcullen, Co. Kildare (see entry below for 24 August).

16　Letter in hand of S, Grey to Walsingham, Dublin (*CSPI* 94.28; reproduced by Plomer [1923] fig. 6): 'The Scots with Con O'Donnel, hearing the strength of the country were assembling, retired. They have altogether spoiled the country of Sligo, and burned the town itself. His revocation toucheth the service.'

28　Letter in hand of S, Grey to Walsingham, Kilmainham [the

sequestered Priory of the Hospitallers which served the Lord Deputy as an alternative temporary base to his permanent residence at Dublin Castle] (*CSPI* 94.46): 'To be favourable to the city of Dublin in their controversy with the customers of Westchester and Helbry.' Letter in hand of S, Grey to Walsingham, Dublin (*CSPI* 94.47): 'Of certain captains' debts to Peter Shurlock, of Waterford, which ought to be paid. That he may have a reversion of the abbey of Cahir, in the county of Tipperary.'

31 Letter in hand of S, Grey to the Privy Council, Kilmainham (*CSPI* 94.61): 'In behalf of Richard Synnott's suits'. Letter addressed by S, Grey to Walsingham, Kilmainham (*CSPI* 94.62): 'His love and favour to the bearer Synnott for his dutiful carriage'.

August

24 S obtains official lease of the dissolved House of Friars Minors, known as New Abbey, Co. Kildare, twenty-five miles from Dublin, one of the forfeited estates of James Eustace, Viscount Baltinglas, who had fled to Spain in 1581. The lease comes 'with an old waste town adjoining, and its appurtenances' (*Fiants*, Eliz. no. 3969): 'Lease under commission 15 July xii) [*sic*] to Edmund Spenser Gent., of the site of the house of friars called New Abbey, Co. Kildare, with appurtenances in the Queens disposition by the rebellion of James Eustace. To hold for 21 years. Rent £3. (Provided he shall not alien to any except they be English both by father or mother, or born in the Pale: and shall not charge coyne or livery. Fine £20).' S is paid by Treasurer Wallop 'for rewards to messengers'. This appears to be the final payment of S's secretaryship for this purpose before Grey's recall.

25 Archbishop Adam Loftus and Henry Wallop appointed Justices of Ireland.

27 Barnaby Googe writes to Burghley from Dublin telling him of a horse which, being consumed by fire in its stable, was then consumed by a hungry mob (*CSPI* 94.98).

29 Paper in hand of S at Dublin (*CSPI* 94.107): 'Certificate of the High Commissioners to Lord Grey, to testify the upright conduct of the bearer John Bird, their Registrar, who has been accused of corrupt dealing.' Marked 'Copia vera, Exr. Ed. Spenser', to which is added, in another hand, 'Secretary to the

Lord Grey, L. Deputy here'. A letter from the Irish privy council to Walsingham indicates that Grey's servants will remain in Ireland to settle his affairs in the wake of the Lord Deputy's departure (*CSPI* 94.106).

31 Grey, recalled, leaves Ireland. End of S's secretaryship.

Proclamation offering general pardon to Munster rebels who submit.

December
3 Richard Synnot's lease of Enniscorthy receives official sanction.

Reference to, or influence of S in the following works: Thomas Blenerhasset, in *A Revelation of the True Minerva*, adopts the verse form of Colin's eulogy in the April Eclogue of *SC* (STC 3132); William Vallans draws on the October Eclogue in his verses in BM Ms. Harleian 367, f. 29.

1583

January
24 Revised version of Stanyhurst's translation of Virgil's *Aeneis* entered in Stationers' Register by Henry Bynneman, publisher of Spenser–Harvey correspondence.

March
11 Bryskett secures reversion of post of Clerk of the Council of Munster upon the death of the holder, Thomas Burgate. The Clerk was also the keeper 'of the signet and of all books, rolls, pleadings, and other records of the presidency court', and attended the Lord President 'in all his employments'.

May
12 S appointed commissioner for musters in Co. Kildare for two years (*Fiants*, Eliz. no. 4150): 'Commission to Henry Cowley Knt' – and 26 others, among them Edmund Spenser of New

Abbey – 'to be commissioners of musters in Co. of Kildare, its crosses and marches; to summon all the subjects of each barony, and then so mustered to assess in warlike apparel, arms, horses, horsemen and footmen, according to the ancient customs and laws of the kingdom and the instructions of the lord justices'. It is worth noting here that a James Spenser later served as Master of Musters in Munster, and was for five years provincial commissioner of Musters in Ireland with William Jones. James Spenser addressed James I on 24 July 1610 (*BL Royal* Ms. 18A.19.275).

August
2   Captain George Thornton succeeds Sir Warham St Leger as provost marshal of Munster.

During this month, S pays rent on New Abbey. This was possibly the only payment he ever made.

October
17   Thomas Burgate dies.
18   From now until 30 April 1584, Bryskett, as formal holder of the Clerkship of Munster, receives 'diet money'. After 30 April 1584, he received only a salary, no diet money.

November
6   Bryskett obtains his Letter Patent under the Great Seal of Ireland for the Clerkship of Munster, at an annual salary of £20. S serves as his deputy, possibly from this date, on a salary of £7 10s (*Liber Munerum Publicorum Hiberniae*, I, ii, p. 187).
11   Earl of Desmond killed near Tralee.

December
12   Bryskett is in London, bearing letters from Adam Loftus, Archbishop of Dublin, and Henry Wallop to Burghley.
31   Under the 'Receiptes and charge' of the Treasurer at Wars in Ireland, Sir Henry Wallop, from 30 September 1588, until 30 September 1591, which also gives 'arrerages' from 1580, there is a 'bill of imprest' (or authorisation to draw money in advance) made out to S under the heading of 'Prestes uppon Enterteynm^{tes}' for £9 6s 8d: 'Bill ultio Decem 1583 by edmond

Spenser Deputy to the said Lodowick briskett, ix^{li} vi^s viii$^{d'}$ (*Ms. Rawl.* A. 317, Bodleian Library, f. 351^v).

Claude Desainliens, *To others that shall happen to write in his commendacion*, verses prefixed to *Campo di Fior, or else the Flourie Field of Foure Languages* (STC 6735), contains possible echo of *SC June* 109. Brian Melbancke, *Philotomus. The Ware betwixt Nature and Fortune* (STC 17801) pp. 12 and 213, draws on *SC Nov* 53 and *Jan* 61.

1584

January
7   Sir John Perrot appointed Lord Deputy of Ireland.
15 The earl of Ormond complains that Bryskett is in England and Henry Shethe, his servant, is deputising. It is not clear whether Bryskett had two deputies, or if S succeeded Shethe.

March
Richard Bingham appointed president of Connaught.

April
30 Bryskett stops receiving diet money, which suggests that he had S serving as his deputy at least from this date.

June
19 Commission to Sir Valentine Browne *et al.* to survey Munster.
24 John Norris appointed president of Munster.

July
4   S again called upon to act as commissioner of musters in Co. Kildare, along with twenty-five others (*Fiants*, Eliz. no. 4464): 'to call before them all the subjects in each barony of the Co. Kildare' etc. as before. 'Return to be made before the last day of August'.
13 John Long becomes Primate of all Ireland.
c.15 S probably accompanies Norris and new Lord Deputy Perrot on tour of inspection through Connaught and Munster to establish Sir Richard Bingham and Sir John Norris in their respective presidencies, returning with company to Dublin via Waterford on receiving news of Sorley Boy MacDonnell

landing on the coast of Antrim at the head of a large body of
Hebridean Scots.

August
25   S leaves Dublin for North Ulster.

September
S probably with Norris, Ormond and the earl of Tyrone when they
siezed 50,000 cattle near Glenconkein in Londonderry and when
they overran Dunluce.

September–November
Survey of forfeited lands in Munster.

October
10   S returns to Dublin.
25   Lord Deputy Perrot writes from Dublin Castle to the Privy
     Council, listing the castles which are to be fortified, including
     S's future home, 'Kilcolman', which is Irish for 'Colman's
     Church'.

November
S accompanies Norris and company of 100 to Munster.
In addition to Bryskett, S's literary acquantances in Dublin include
Geoffrey Fenton, Barnaby Rich, and Barnaby Googe.
   References to S in the following works: Thomas Lodge, *An
Alarum against Usurers. Containing tryed experiences against worldly
abuses* (STC 16653), *truths Complaint Over England*, Sig. L, contains
an echo of *SC Nov* 53; George Peele, *The Araygnement of Paris. A
Pastorall* (STC 19530) act 3, scene 1, sig. Cij and scene 2, sig. Ciij,
contains references to *SC*.

1585

March
1   S and Norris back in Dublin.
7   Letters in hand of S, John Norris to the Privy Council, Dublin
    (*CSPI* 115.13): 'The Lord Deputy being discounselled from the
    Ulster journey, Norreys returns to his province. The wasteness
    and general desolation of his province is such, as well for

want of people as of cattle, being all consumed through the late wars, as that amongst them, which remain many stealths are committed to keep them in life, which are hard to be avoided through their extreme necessity'; John Norris to the Privy Council, Dublin (*CSPI* 115.14): 'Commends Mr. Lambert for his valour and manly behaviour. His necessities to be relieved'; John Norris to Burghley, Dublin (*CSPI* 115.15): 'Mr. Lambert, through his maims, utterly disabled from helping himself'; John Norris to Walsingham, Dublin (*CSPI* 115.16): 'The bold and valiant carriage of Mr. Lambert in the encounter with the Scots.'

31 Letter in hand of S, John Norris to Burghley, Clonmel (*CSPI* 115.41): 'The wasteness of his province is so huge and universal for want of people that it will be very long before the inhabitants shall regain any ability of living. The Lord Deputy has assigned him the custodiam of Moally and Tralee, but will not dispossess Captain Barkley of Askeaton. His suits for land. Victual. The soldier to find himself. He has taken two pirates, and would take more if the Lord Deputy would pay his charge out of the prizes taken'. Document in hand of S, 'Note of Desmond lands' (*CSPI* 115.42): 'Note of some of the late Earl of Desmond's lands, which the Lord President John Norreys thinks most fit to be laid to the presidentship of Munster, and also of some which he desires for himself in fee simple.'

April
26 Opening of Irish Parliament. John Norris represents Cork and Thomas Norris represents Limerick in this session of parliament.

June
23 Walsingham notes that 'Mr. John Norris is presently to take 3000 foot and 200 horse into the Low Countries' (*CSPF*, 1584–5, p. 537).

December
Scheme for Munster plantation drawn up.

John Dove, *Poimenologia, que vulgo calendarium pastorum e versu Anglicano in latium traducta. Huic accessit epicedium sub nomine Iakues pastoris, in obitum Algrindi archipoimenos, de quo toties occurit mentio in hoc libro*, MS translation of *SC* at Gonville and Caius College (*Catalogue of MSS at the Library of Gonville and Caius College*, Cambridge, 1908, 2.627). Dove ascribes the poem to an unknown author; 'ut hoc opusculum jam pene deletum et quasi sepultum, de novo vestrae lectioni secundo commendarum'.

1586

Between Autumn 1585 and spring of this year, S must have attended the sessions of the presidency court of Munster at Limerick and Cork.

January
6   Wallop writes to Walsingham of his plans for developing 360 acres of the lands of Enniscorthy leased from Synnot for £150. Wallop did not receive the official lease until 1595 (*Fiants*, Eliz. no. 5963).

February
27   S once more in Dublin.

March
4   Kilcolman 'taken' by Andrew Reade, possibly acting on behalf of S, who in May seems to claim the estate.

April
26   Opening of Irish parliament. Sir Thomas Norris, acting President of Munster while brother John is fighting in the Netherlands, represents Munster in the Irish Parliament for this session. S almost certainly in attendance throughout.

May
8   Irish parliament passes act nullifying all conveyances. The earl of Desmond had conveyed his possessions to James Butler, Baron of Dunboyne, on 10 September 1572, in order to ward off confiscation. S roundly condemned such 'colourable conveyances' in the *View*.
11   Some knights and burgesses attempt to obstruct passage through Irish parliament of acts of attainder, designed to

facilitate Munster plantation. S has Irenius in the *View* say 'howe hardlie that acte was wrounge out of them, I cann wytnes: and were yt to be compassed againe, I dare undertake it would never be compassed'.

14 End of session of Irish parliament.

June

27 Articles for the Munster Undertakers receive the royal assent. The Queen's letter conveys the escheated land in County Cork to 'Sr Walter Rawleigh Sr John Stawell & Sr John Peyton knightes their associates and the gentlemen Undertakers of the counties of Devon Som^rset and Dorsett and such others as shall be joyned unto them in societie.' No mention of S.

July

5 Treaty of Berwick between Scots and English.

18 S dates sonnet to Harvey from Dublin, published in Harvey's *Foure Letters* in 1592.

September

2 Sir Thomas Norris appointed one of the commissioners for the survey of attainted lands. A total of 63,000 acres surveyed in the coming winter. Kilcolman described as 'a large castle, old, and dilapidated, which at the present time has no use except to shelter cattle in the night'. It is likely that S, when he took up residence, lived in a house on the estate, and not in the castle itself.

22 Bingham massacres Scots supporters of Mayo Burkes at Ardnaree.

S probably attended sessions of presidency court of Munster which met in latter half of this month at Dungarvon and the first half of October at Lismore and Youghal to allot immense seignories to Sir Christopher Hatton and Sir Walter Raleigh. For the remainder of the winter S resides in Cork. From now until he leaves Ireland with Raleigh in 1589, S is intimately involved with the complex business of the Munster plantation.

October

17 Death of Philip Sidney at Arnhem in the Low Countries.

December

8 S delinquent in payment of first fruits, a sum required of the occupant of a benefice upon taking his charge, with respect to the prebendary of Effin, possibly a sinecure post (*CSPI* 127.18): 'Book containing the following pieces: – Proceedings by information in the Exchequer against the Bishop of Meath, Doctor Conway and Robert Draper, parson of Trim. – Note of such Bishops and others as are sued for double fruits upon the Statute 26. Hen. VIII. j Collection of the arrearages of first fruits. These contain the names of many of the clergy of the time, amongst others James Weslye, vicar of Maynam; Edmondus Spenser, prebendary of Effin; and Thaddaeus Dowlinge, treasurer of Leighlin.' A prebend was an endowment in land or pension in money given to a cathedral for maintenance of a secular priest or regular canon. Effin, west of Balingaddy, a prebendary attached to Limerick Cathedral, comprised about 1,052 acres of land. In *MHT* (ll. 414–17) S had satirised unqualified holders of clerical offices:

> How manie honest men see ye arize
> Daylie thereby, and grow to goodly prize;
> To Deanes, to Archdeacons; to Commissaries,
> To Lords, to Principalls, to Prebendaries?

17 Richard Beacon appointed attorney general of Munster on a salary of £13 6s 8d per annum.

Publication of *SC*, third edition, London.

Reference to S in the following work: William Webbe, *A Discourse of English Poetrie* (*STC* 25172), Sigs. Ciiii[v]–D, writes in praise of *SC*: 'This place have I purposely reserved for one, who if not only, yet in my judgement principally deserveth the tytle of the rightest English Poet, that ever I read: that is, the Author of the Sheepeheardes Kalender, intituled to the woorthy Gentleman Master *Phillip Sidney*: whether it was Master *Sp.* or what rare Scholler in Pembroke Hall soever, because himself and his freendes, for what respect I knowe not, would not reveale it, I force not greatly to sette downe.'

1587

February
8 Mary Stuart executed.
16 Wallop and the other Irish Commissioners write to Burghley (*CSPI* 128.44): 'in the course of the official survey of the lands of the Munster Undertakers Arthur Robyns, surveyor, has recently made a survey of "Killcolman"'.
28 Order granting Sir Walter Raleigh 3½ seignories (42,000 acres) in Cos. Cork and Waterford.

March
14 Kilcolman assigned to 'Andrew Reade of faccombe within the county of Southa[mpton] gente' (*Carew* Ms. 632, no. 10). There is no evidence to suggest that Reade ever occupied his lands.

S in Cork for spring session of Munster council.

April
26 Andrew Reade appointed one of a 'commission for hearing and ending controversies between the Undertakers' (*CSPI* 129.26).

June
S in Limerick for summer session of Munster council. Remainder of summer spent in Cork, Kilmallock, and Clonmel.

September
4 Kilcolman confirmed as assigned by the Commissioners to 'Andrew Reade of Facombe, Co. Southampton, gent.'

October
1 S officially serving as deputy to Bryskett, Clerk of the Council of Munster. Henceforth it is likely that a deputy undertook S's duties at the Court of Chancery until that office was sold.

November
S in Limerick for autumn session of Munster council.

December

18 Andrew Reade is mentioned in a letter from Popham as having been allotted the estate of Kilcolman (*CSPI* 132.39).

Publication of the first edition of Camden's *Britannia*. Angell Daye, *Daphnis and Chloe interlaced with the praises of a most peerlesse Princesse, wonderful in Majestie, and rare in perfection, celebrated within the same Pastorall, and therefore termed by the name of The Shepheards Holidaie* (*STC* 6400, ed. Joseph Jacobs, 1890) pp. 36–7, echoes *SC Apr* 37–153. About this time, George Whetstone, in *Sir Phillip Sidney, his honorable life, his valiant death, and true vertues* (*STC* 25349), Sig. B 2^v, wrongly attributes *SC* to Sidney.

1588

S in Cork for the first half of this year. S was probably a regular visitor at Raleigh's house of the College of Youghal, called the Wardens. Raleigh was Mayor of Youghal at this time, and Sir Thomas Norris obtained a lease of the College, where he resided.

February

16 Lord Roche writes to the earl of Ormond complaining that the undertakers seek to rob him of his lands by means of 'untrue inquisitions'.

17 Sir William Fitzwilliam reappointed Lord Deputy.

About twenty-five ships of the defeated Spanish Armada wrecked off Irish coast.

March

31 Salary of Clerkship of Munster entered as usual to Bryskett. Underneath the entry is a marginal note, written by William Sandes, deputy to the Clerk of the Check: 'This is exercised by one Spenser as deputy to the said Bryskett to whom it was granted by patent 6th Nov. 25 Eliz.' (*Cal. Carew MSS*, 1575–88, p. 462).

June

11 Abraham Fraunce's *Arcadian Rhetorike*, in which *FQ* II iv 35 is quoted, entered in the Stationers' Register.

22 S sells post of Clerk of Court of the Chancery for faculties to
    Arland Uscher, to whom the patent is passed.

July
1   Letter in hand of S, Thomas Norris to Walsingham, Limerick
    (*CSPI* 135.66; first page reproduced by Jenkins, [1938] p. 350):
    'Mr Vice-President of Munster, Thomas Norreys, to Secretary
    Walsyngham. Manner in which Florence McCarthy compassed
    the marriage with the Earl of Clancar's daughter. Grounds of
    his cunning dealings. Captain Jacques privy to his intentions
    before he left England. Florence McCarthy's affinity with the
    house of James Fitzmaurice. His purchase of the Old Head of
    Kinsale. Florence McCarthy, the Countess of Clancar, Mc-
    Finnin, and others committed. *Seal with arms.*'

September
3   Earliest date on which S may have occupied Kilcolman. Lord
    Roche complains to the Queen's Commissioners that certain of
    his lands have been occupied by the Undertakers.

October
1   S as part of retinue of vice-president Thomas Norris must
    have left Cork on military expedition against Spaniards who
    survived in Connaught and Ulster after the wreck of the
    Armada.

November
c.15 S with Norris when he unites with newly appointed Deputy
    Sir William Fitzwilliam at Sligo.
24 Combined English forces arrive at Ballyshannon in Con-
    naught.

December
At the end of this month S is in Dublin to see Thomas Norris
knighted by Fitzwilliam.
   Reference to, or influence of S in the following works: Abraham
Fraunce, *The Arcadian Rhetorike: Or The Praecepts of Rhetorike made
plaine by examples, Greeke, Latin, English, French, Spanish,* Sig. E 3,
quotes *FQ* II iv 35, citing the proper Book and Canto. That *FQ* was
circulating in manuscript is also shown by Marlowe's borrowings
in 2 *Tamburlaine* (1590, written about 1587). Fraunce also quotes *SC*

Aug 151-62 on sig. D 7ᵛ, and on sig. C 4 he quotes the twenty-one-line *Iambicum Trimetrum* of the Spenser-Harvey correspondence, beginning 'Unhappie verse the witnes of my unhappie state.' Fraunce is the first to name S as author of *SC*. Fraunce makes contant allusions to *SC* in *The Lawiers Logike, exemplifying the praecepts of Logike by the practise of the Common Lawe* (STC 11343). Henry Lyte, *The Light of Britayne. A Recorde of the honorable Originall & Antiquitie of Britaine*, sig. A 4, refers to Elizabeth as 'Britomartis'.

1589

S must have attended the spring and summer sessions of the Munster Council.

January
Early in the New Year, S sets out with Norris for Munster.

22   Letter in hand of S, Thomas Norris to the Privy Council, Shandon Castle, Cork (*CSPI* 140.37): 'Your Lordships' letters dated at Greenwich the 21st of last December, I received on the 12th of January as I was on my way from Dublin into Munster. Your letters import some doubt of the arrival of Sir William Stanley in Munster, who, as your Lordships were informed, was with his own regiment, and some other forces ready to embark at Dunkirk, for some secret attempt intended against these parts, for the withstanding of whom I will apply myself with the small forces which Her Majesty has in this province. And, where your Lordships seem to conceive some special doubt of the fort of Duncannon, upon the river of Waterford, as a place dangerous both for harbouring of a great number of ships, and also for offending of other parts adjoining, which place was last year begun by Sir John Perrot to be fortified, and yet not finished, I have endeavoured to carry out your directions; but inasmuch as I have not sufficient means and as the place is outside the precinct of the province of Munster, now under my charge, I have made known your Lordships' pleasure to the Lord Deputy. And as for the aids of the country here which your Lordships wish to be put in a readiness, although hitherto I have forborne to impart any intelligence or doubt of foreign invasion unto them, knowing how prone and ready they ever be to entertain

their vain hopes of popish succour, yet now I will frame some other colourable occasion whereby to draw such of the noblemen and better sort of gentlemen, whom I think best affected towards Her Majesty, to be at all times in a reasonable readiness to rise out to meet any such accident of foreign arrival if it shall happen. As the province now is, Sir William Stanley, with such small forces as he is able to bring with him, shall find so weak a party here to join with him, as that he shall not be able to compass anything which may breed any sudden hazard. A further supply of ammunition is wanted. In former letters your Lordships often signified that for the better support of the presidency here, some escheated lands should be united to the place, and thereupon Carrighroghan with some other small things was appointed for that purpose. I think it right to remind your Lordships of this, knowing how difficult it is here for maintenance of "stable needments" and other household provisions, for which it is very hard here otherwise to make purveyance, and whereof here is most need, but Carrighroghan is now claimed by Sir Richard Grenvil as a part of Kirrywhirrhy. To avoid such difficulties it would be well to set down some such establishment of that place and of the rest, unto this government, as might take away all doubts and demands.

Upon my return out of the late northern journey I found this province in reasonable good conditions of peace and tranquillity, but some of the Undertakers have been very disorderly of late, thrust themselves into other men's lands, and taken castles, the which were not formerly escheated nor found by office to Her Majesty, through whose disordered doings the country people conceive great discontentment as they have cause. When I seek to redress these things I doubt not but I shall be reported to your Lordships as a hinderer of that action, which otherwise I further and favour. It might be well if your Lordships let the said Undertakers know that it would be better for them to fashion themselves to live within compass of law, and to measure their actions by the rule thereof as in England they have been accustomed.'

February
Early this month, the townspeople of Munster gathered in their respective cathedrals for a special thanksgiving for the English

victory over the Armada. S probably in Cork to hear Bishop Lyons deliver a sermon before a congregation of 2,000.

16   The Anglo-Irish noble, Maurice, Lord Roche of Fermoy, a neighbour of S, complains of his lands being siezed by the undertakers, including S. S's other Cork neighbours include Lord David Barry, William Synan, and his wife, Ellen Butler.

17   Lease for New Abbey passed to Thomas Lambyn.

March

4   S in process of trying to secure Kilcolman for himself. An official letter, 'A true declaration concerning the undertakers in Cork, by Sir John Popham', notes that 'Mr Reade hath taken Kilcolman being about 3000 acres, but what he hath done in it I know not' (*CSPI* 142.10).

24   S has occupied Kilcolman by this date.

May

22   S obtains official possession of Kilcolman, 3,000 acres, paying around £20 annual rent. Establishes a colony of six house-holders with their families.

Commission to inquire into progress of Munster plantation. Document in hand of S detailing his answers to the Articles (*CSPI* 144.70):

> The answer of Edmund Spenser, gent. to the articles of Instructions given in charge to the Commissioners for examining and inquiring of Her Majesty's attainted lands past to the undertakers.
>   1. To the first he saith that he hath undertaken the peopling of a seignory of 4,000 acres allotted unto him by a particular from the undertakers, in which the castle and lands of Kilcolman and Rossack were appointed unto him, the which want much of the said whole proportion of 4,000 acres.
>   2. To the second he saith he hath not as yet passed his patent of the said lands, but so soon as Justice Smythes, who is only left now of the quorum, returns from England the patent will be passed.

3. To the third he saith that there wanteth his due proportion 1,000 acres as he supposed at the least.

4. To the fourth, fifth and sixth he knoweth of chargeable lands and chief-rents within the compass of his particular, but only four nobles upon Ballinegarragh and 6/8 upon Ballinfoynigh.

5. To the seventh and eighth he saith that as yet he hath not made any division of his lands to his tenants, for that his patent is not yet passed unto him, nor his lands established.

6. To the ninth, tenth and eleventh he saith that he hath hitherto but six households of English people upon his land for the former causes.

7. To the twelfth he saith that sundry honest persons in England have promised to come over to inhabit his land as soon as his patent is [passed].

S had entered into an arrangement with Andrew Reade whereby Kilcolman would belong to the former if none of Reade's relatives came to claim it by Whitsuntide (22 May) 1589.

October

12 Lord Roche writes from Castle Town to Elizabeth detailing complaints and indicting S (*CSPI* 147.14–15): 'M.de Rupe and Fermoy, i.e., Lord Roche to Queen Elizabeth. Complains of injuries done to him and his tenants by the undertakers. He is like to be dispossessed of his ancient inheritance. He relies on Her Majesty's promise past when he took leave of Her Majesty'.

'M. de Rupe and Fermoy, i.e., the Lord Roche, to Walsyngham. Wishes the inclosed to be laid before the Queen'.

'Particulars of injuries done to the Lord Roche by Edmund Spenser [the Poet] Clerk of the Council in Munster, George Browne, Hugh Cuffe, Justice Smythes and Arthur Hyde. Edmund Spenser falsely pretending title to certain castles and 16 ploughlands, hath taken possession thereof. Also, by threatening and menacing the said Lord Roche's tenants, and by siezing their cattle, and beating Lord Roche's servants and bailiffs he has wasted 6 ploughlands of his Lordship's lands.'

The specific charges against S read: 'An[n]o 1588. ffurther one Edmonde Spenser clearke of the counsel in mounster by collo[r] of his office and by makinge of corrupt Bargaines w[th] certaine psons pretendinge falslie title to p[ar]cell of the L. Roches laundes dispossed the said L. Roch of certaine castles and xvi plough laundes. Allsoe the said Spenser by threathninge and manacinge of the said L. Roch [h]is ten[an]ts and by takinge theire cattaile pasturinge uppon his L[ordshi]ps owne inheritance and by refusinge and beatinge of his L[ordshi]ps serivantes, and Balives hath made waste six other ploughe laundes of his L[ordshi]ps laufull inheritance to his noe small undoinge'.

Bill against the Lord Roche by S and others, including fellow undertaker, Hugh Cuffe, autographed with endorsement by S (*CSPI* 147.16): 'Bill against the Lord Roche. He relieved one Kedagh O'Kelly, his foster brother, a proclaimed traitor, has imprisoned men of Mr. Verdon's, Mr. Edmund Spenser and others. He speaks ill of Her Majesty's government and hath uttered words of contempt of Her Majesty's laws, calling them unjust. He killed a fat beef of Teig Olyve's, because Mr. Spenser lay in his house one night as he came home from the sessions at Limerick. He also killed a beef of his smith's for mending Mr. Peers's plough iron. He has forbidden his people to have any trade or conference with Mr. Spenser or Mr. Piers or their Tenants. He has concealed from Her Majesty the manor of Crogh, being the freehold of one who was a rebel.' There was an order made at Waterford (*CPSI* 147.247.17): 'Order passed, by Sir Thomas Norreys, Sir Robert Gardener, &c., commissioners for the titles in Munster, against Lord Roche. The defendants Jesse Smythes and Robert Ashfield to continue their possessions. Copy under the hand of Robert Tyrry, Deputy Clerk of the Crown, Munster.'

29 A note on 'The proceedings of the undertakers in Munster' mentions S (*CSPI* 147.51.I) [Entry Book, Ireland, Folios vol. 12, p. 291. no. 2]: 'The proceedings of the Undertakers in Munster' (p. 258) 'Mr Edmond Spenser hath by particular 4,000 acres. . . . Totals: – Acres, 178, 845: rent, 1, 933l. 0s. 7½d., and 159 kine. Inhabitants. English, 536; Irish not set down'.

Visit of Raleigh to Kilcolman as recorded in *Colin Clout*. Leaving a substitute deputy, 'one Chitester' (Richard Chichester), S returns to

England with Raleigh, and has a private audience with Queen Elizabeth, who reportedly took delighted in *FQ* 'and it desir'd at timely houres to hear'.

December
1   *FQ* entered in Stationers' Register: 'a booke intytuled *the fayrye Queene dysposed into xii. bookes, Etc'*.

Undated document in hand of S (*BM Add. Ms.* 19869): 'Grant from Edmund Spenser to McHenry (a junior member of the Roche family), of the Custody of the Woods of Balliganim, &c., county Cork, Ireland': 'Be it knowen to all men by these presents, that I Edmund Spenser of Kilcolman esqu. doe give unto McHenry the keping of all the woodes which I have in Balliganim, and of the rushes and brakes, without making any spoyle thereof, and also doe covenaunt with him, that he shall have one house within the bawne of Richardston for himself and his cattell in tyme of warre. And also within the space of vij yeares to repayre the castle of Richardston aforesayd, and in all other thinges to us[e] good neighbourhood to him and his, signed: Edmund Spenser'.

Reference to or influence of S in the following works: William Byrd, *Songs of sundrie natures* (STC 4256) no. 23, writes in the Spenserian manner. See *SC Dec* 1–2, *Gn.* 237–8; *Col.* 56–60. Robert Greene, *Menaphon* (STC 12272), sig. Hᵛ, echoes *FQ* III vi 6. Thomas Lodge, *Scillas Metamorphosis: Enterlaced with the unfortunate love of Glaucus* (STC 16674), contains numerous echoes of *SC* and *FQ*. Thomas Nashe, *To the Gentlemen of both Universities*, prefixed to Robert Greene's *Menophon* (STC 12272) sig. A 2–A 2ᵛ, writes thus of pastoral poems: 'and should the challenge of deepe conceit, be intruded by any forreiner, to bring our english wits, to the tutcsthone of Arte, I would preferre, divine Master *Spencer*, the miracle of wit to bandie line for line for my life, in the honour of *England*, gainst *Spaine*, *France*, *Italie*, and all the worlde'. George Peele, *A Farewell. Entituled to . . . Sir John Norris & Sir Francis Drake . . . Whereunto is annexed: a tale of Troy* (STC 19537) sig. B, echoes *SC Apr* 33–6. Peele also draws on S in *An Eglogue. Gratulatorie Entituled: To . . . Robert Earle of Essex* (STC 19534), with use of characters *Piers* and *Palinode* and adoption of same rustic dialect. George Puttenham, *The Arte of English Poesie* (STC 20519) p. 51, recommends: 'For Eglogue and pastorall Poesie, Sir *Philip*

Sydney and Maister *Challener*, and that other Gentleman who wrate
the late shepheardes Callender.'

1590

January
23 S's 'Letter to Raleigh' dated from Kilcolman, appended to *FQ*
    I–III.

May
6   Elizabeth, by letters patent under the Great Seal of Ireland,
    grants S and his heirs forever in fee-farm the manor, castle,
    town and lands of Kilcolman, with a clause to the effect that
    after the Feast of St Michael, 1594, upon the death of any
    tenant of any principal habitation or any alteration thereof,
    'his or their best beast' should be reserved to the Crown, for
    and in the name of a heriot. Upon S's death, 'or that of all his
    heirs or assigns, a relief should be paid according to the
    custom, &c., of England' (*Memoranda Roll of the Irish Exchequer*,
    James I, 1606, membrane 39).
8   Mention of 'one Chitester' (Richard Chichester) serving as
    substitute for S 'in his office of clerkship of Munster', possibly
    while S was in England (*CSPI* 152.15): 'Richard Whyte to
    Burghley – on evil conditions of Ireland – that many English
    in office there are papists. "In the beginning of last Lent Sir
    Thomas Norreys, in Limerick, came to the Lord's Table, but
    not one of his gentlemen came thither except one Chitester
    [Chichester] substitute to Mr. Spenser in his office of Clerkship
    of Munster".'
30 Under the 'Receiptes and charge' of the Treasurer at Wars in
    Ireland, Sir Henry Wallop, from 30 September 1588, until 30
    September 1591, there is a 'bill of imprest' made out to S for £6
    13s 4d (MS Rawl. A.317, f. 351^v): 'Bill xxx^{mo} Maij 1590 by y^e
    said Spenser vi^{li} xiii^s. iiij^d.' It is not clear whether the bill was
    made out to S in person. If it was, S may have returned briefly
    to Ireland, possibly to handle law suits with Lord Roche. This
    is a year that S is otherwise generally assumed to have spent
    largely in England.

July

6   Bryskett paid £6 13s 4d as Clerk of the Council of Munster (MS Rawl. A.317, f. 351ᵛ): 'Bill vjᵗᵒ die Julij 1590 by the said Bryskett vjⁱⁱ xiiijˢ iiijᵈ.'

October

26   S receives royal grant 'for ever, in fee farm' of Kilcolman: 'Grant (English) to Edmund Spenser, gentleman, of the manor, castle and lands of Kylcolman, Co. Cork, containing one ploughland, Kylnevalley, 1 pl., Lysnemucky, 1 pl., Ard Adam, 1 pl., Arden-reagh, Ould Rossack alias Croscack 1pl., Carrigyne, 1 pl., Bally Ellis, 1 pl., Kyllmack Ennes, ½ pl., and Ardenbane, ½ pl., Co. Cork, amounting by measure to 3028 English acres; also a rent of 26s 8d due to the late lord of Thitmore, out of Ballymacadam, and a rent of 6s. 8d., payable to the late traitor, Sir John of Desmond, out of Ballynloynigh, Co. Cork. To hold for ever, in fee farm, by the name of 'Hap Hazard' by fealty, in common socage. Rent, £17 7s. 6d. from 1594 (half only for the previous three years) and 33s. 4d. for service of the free tenants. Also ½d. for each acre of waste land enclosed. If the lands are found by the survey to contain more than the estimated number of acres, grantee shall pay 1d. for each English acre in excess. Power to impark 151 acres. Grantee to build houses for 24 families, of which one to be for himself, 2 for freeholders of 300a., 2 for farmers of 400a., and 11 for copyholders of 100a. Other conditions usual in the grants to the undertakers in Munster' (*Cal. Fiants*, Eliz. 5473). Evidence from the Irish Court of Exchequer indicates that S was initially charged an annual fee farm rent of £9 10s 5¾d on Kilcolman (Ferguson's 'Memorials').

December

29   *Comp.* entered in Stationers' Register.

Publication of *FQ*, books I–III. Commendatory poems by Raleigh and others. The ten dedicatory sonnets addressed to leading noble families in England and Ireland increased to seventeen in later copies. Since S dedicates *FQ* to Elizabeth, he may have presented a copy to her. Publication of Philip Sidney's *Old Arcadia*. Publication of Robert Payne's *A Brife Description of Ireland*, London.

Sometime between now and 1594 *John of Bordeaux or The Second*

Part of Friar Bacon (Alnwick Castle MS) shows general influence of
SC. Thomas Lodge, *Rosalynde. Euphues golden legacie* (*STC* 16664),
alludes to Lodge's projected *Sailers Kalender*, probably inspired by
SC. Christopher Marlowe, *Tamburlaine the Greate . . . Devided into
two Tragicall Discourses* (*STC* 17425), contains numerous echoes of
FQ. See for example part I, I.ii.393: '*Jove* sometime masked in a
Shepheards weed.' Compare *FQ* I, proem i, 1–2. William Vallens, *A
Tale of Two Swannes. Wherein is comprehended the original and increase
of the river Lee commonly called Ware-river: together, with the antiquitie
of sundrie places and townes seated upon the same* (*STC* 24590),
contains allusions to *Epith., FQ* and *SC*. Thomas Watson, *An
Eglogue Upon the death of the Right Honorable Sir Francis Walsingham*
(*STC* 25121), sig. C 3^v – C 4, praises S.

1591

February
25 S granted a life pension of £50 a year by Elizabeth (*Cal. Pat.
Roll 33 Eliz.*).

March
11 Founding of Trinity College, Dublin.
13 First stone of the new university laid by Thomas Smith, Mayor
of Dublin.

July
10 Richard Chichester again noted as occupying post of deputy
clerk of Munster for S.

September
Bryskett is still receiving the emoluments of his office of Clerk of
the Council of Munster – £20 sterling per annum – this month (MS
Rawl. A.317, f. 62).

October
Fourth edition of *SC* entered in Stationers' Register.

December
20 Richard Beacon surrenders his office of attorney general of
Munster.

27 S's *Col.*, published in 1595, dated from 'my house at Kilcolman'.

Publication of fourth edition of *SC*. Publication of S's *Comp.*, 'being all complaints and meditations of the worlds vanitie, verie grave and profitable': *The Ruines of Time, The Teares of the Muses, Virgils Gnat* (a version of the pseudo-Virgilian *Culex*), *Prosopopoia* or *Mother Hubberds Tale, The Ruines of Rome: by Bellay* (trans. from the *Antique de Rome*), *Muiopotmos: or the Fate of the Butterflie* (dated 1590), *Visions of the Worlds Vanitie*, and also *The Visions of Bellay* and *The Visions of Plutarch: formerly translated* (revised from van der Noot's *Theatre for Worldlings*, 1569). Part of *Comp.* was suppressed, possibly due to the satire in *MHT*, taken to be directed at Burghley, noted by Harvey: 'Mother Hubbard in heat of choller, forgetting the pure sanguine of her sweete Faery Queene, wilfully over-shott her malcontented selfe.' The publisher, Ponsonby, expressed his desire to publish other works by S: '*Ecclesiastes*, and *Canticum canticorum* translated, *A senights slumber* [cf. *My Slomber*, under 1580], *The hell of lovers, his Purgatorie* . . . *The Dying Pellicane* [see under 1580], *The howers of the Lord, The sacrifice of a sinner, The seven Psalmes* [cf. *Petrarch's seven penitentiall psalmes*, trans. Chapman, 1612]'. None of these poems have survived.

Reference to or influence of S in the following works: Thomas Bradshaw, *The Shepherds Starre* (STC 3508), perhaps influenced by *SC*; John Florio, *Florios Second Frutes* (STC 11097), *The Epistle Dedicatorie*, sig. A 3–A 3ᵛ, praises S and his past patron, the Earl of Leicester; Sir John Harington, *Orlando Furioso in English Heroical Verse* (STC 746), p. 373, alludes to 'M. *Spencers* tale of the squire of Dames, in his excellent Poem of the Faery Queene, in the end of vij. Canto of the third booke'; Thomas Nashe, in his Preface to Sidney's *Astrophel and Stella* (STC 22536), makes possible reference to *Comp.*

1592

January

1 Publication of S's *Daphnaida. An Elegie upon the death of the noble and vertuous Douglas Howard, Daughter of Lord Howard and wife of Arthur Gorges*. Dated from London. An imitation of Chaucer's *Book of the Duchess*.

February

15 John Ashfield obtains his grant for the post of attorney general of Munster recently vacated by Beacon.

March

3 Charter incorporating Trinity College, Dublin.

May

1 *Axiochus* entered in the Stationers' Register.

August–September

S 'absent' from his estate and from Cork. Possibly in England. Suspected, with others, of not having well 'performed the plot of the habitation' (*CSPI* 167.44.V).

September

2 S's assignees of Enniscorthy.

December

31 S mentioned several times in a report on Munster undertakers sent from Dublin by Sir Robert Gardener and Roger Wilbraham to Burghley (*CSPI* 167.44.III): 'An abstract or brief particular of all the names of the undertakers, the several counties, the quantity of their lands and their yearly rents, in Munster . . . Cork, Edmund Spenser hath of rentable lands the number of 3,028 acres, redditus inde per annum a festo Michaelis, 1591, pro tribus annis, 8l. 13s. 9d., et a festo Michaelis, 1594, per annum exinde im perpetuum 17l. 7s. 6½d. Chief rents 1l. 13s. 4d. . . . The names of such undertakers within the province as have paid their several rents reserved upon their letters patent into Her Majesty's receipt of Exchequer due at the Feasts of Easter and Michaelmas, 1592, viz . . . Cork, Edmund Spenser, 15l. 15s. 10d. . . . An abstract of the proceedings of the undertakers in Munster, showing the number of acres, the Queen's rent, the number of Irish families inhabiting upon each seignory. . . . Mr. Edmund Spenser hath by particular only 4,000 acres, the rent 22l.' S also appears in a list of undertakers who have paid their rents to the exchequer (*CSPI* 167.44.IV): 'Cork, Edmund Spenser, 3l. 19s. 6d. at Michaelmas'.

Publication of the pseudo-Platonic *Axiochus. A most excellent Dialogue, written in Greek by Plato the Phylosopher*, trans. by *Edw. Spenser*. From a Latin translation. S's involvement in this publication has been questioned by eminent Spenserians, including A. C. Hamilton.

Reference to, or influence of S in the following works: About this time, Walter Raleigh's *The 11th: and last booke of the Ocean to Scinthia* (Hatfield MS, Cecil Papers, 144), echoes *FQ*: 'a Queen she was to mee, no more Belphebe'. Nicholas Breton, *The Pilgrimage to Paradise, joyned with the Countesse of Penbrookes love* (STC 3683), contains echoes of *Col.* Samuel Daniel, *Delia. Contayning certayne Sonnets: with the complaint of Rosamond* (STC 6253), contains echoes of *SC*, for example Sonnet II, sig. B^v:

> Goe wailing verse, the infants of my love,
> Minerva-like, brought foorth without a Mother:
> Present the image of the cares I prove,
> Witnes your Fathers griefe exceeds all other.

Compare S's verses *To his Booke* at the opening of *SC*. There is a reference to *MHT* in the anonymous pamphlet *A Declaration of the True Causes of the Great Troubles, Presupposed to be intended against the realme of England* (STC 10005) p. 68, which is critical of Burghley. Abraham Fraunce, *The Third Part of the Countesse of Pembrokes Iuychurch: Entituled Amintas Dale* (STC 11341), sig. N^v, quotes *SC Mar* 94–102. Gabriel Harvey, *Foure Letters and Ceratine Sonnets* (STC 12900), contains numerous references to S, and to *FQ* and *MHT*. Thomas Nashe, *Pierce Penilesse His Supplication to the Divell* (STC 18371-3) pp. 39–40, gently chides Spenser for failing to include a dedicatory sonnet in *FQ* to 'a piller of Nobilitie', possibly the Earl of Derby. Nashe again refers to S, disparaging Harvey, in *Strange Newes, Of the intercepting certaine Letters, and a Convoy of Verses, as they were going Privilie to victuall the Low Countries* (STC 18377-7^a), sig. E–E^v: 'Immortal *Spencer*, no frailtie hath thy fame, but the imputation of this Idiots friendship: upon an unspotted *Pegasus* should thy gorgeous attired *Fayrie Queene* ride triumphant through all reports dominions, but that this mud-born bubble, this bile on the browe of the Universitie, this bladder of pride newe blowne, challengeth some interest in her prosperitie.'

1593

Nicholas Curtis apparently purchases the office of deputy clerk of Munster from S in this year. Lord Roche petitions the Lord Chancellor of Ireland, Adam Loftus: 'Whereas, one Edmund Spenser, gentleman, hath lately exhibited suit against your suppliant for three plowe lands, parcell of Shanballymore (east of Doneraile), your suppliant's inheritance, before the Vice-President and Councill of Munster, which land hath bene heretofore decreed for your suppliant against the said Spenser and others under whom he conveied; and, nevertheless, for that the said Spenser, being clark of the council in the said province, and did assyne his office unto one Nicholas Carteys, among other agreements, with covenant that during his life he should be free in the said office for his causes etc.' At the same time, Roche presented a petition against Joan Ny Callaghan on the basis of that person's 'supportation and mayntenance of Edmond Spenser, gentleman, a heavy adversary unto your suppliant'.

January
9   First student admitted to Trinity College, Dublin.

October
Death of Lord Grey. This event may have prompted the defense of Lord Grey in book V of *FQ*.

Reference to, or influence of S in the following works: Barnabe Barnes, *Parthenophil and Parthenope* (*STC* 1469), contains allusions to *SC*. See Canzon 2, st. 8.6–7 and Ode 7, st. 2.1–2. Thomas Churchyard, *Churchyards Challenge* (*STC* 5220), sig. **v, praises S thus:

> Then gentle world I sweetly thee beseech:
> Call *Spenser* now the spirit of learned speech.

Michael Drayton, *Idea. The Shepheards Garland, Fashioned in nine Eglogs* (*STC* 7202), contains many echoes of *SC*. Gabriel Harvey, in *A New Letter of Notable Contents* (*STC* 12902), sig. 4 4ᵛ, asks: 'is not the Verse of M. *Spencer* in his brave Faery Queene, the Virginall of the divinest Muses, and the gentlest Graces?' Harvey's *Pierces Supererogation or A New Prayse of The Old Asse* cites a sonnet by

Barnabe Barnes addressed to Harvey in which the dedicatee is praised for his association with S. Harvey makes repeated use of S's name in his attack on Thomas Nashe. Thomas Lodge, *Phillis: Honoured with Pastorall Sonnets, Elegies, and amorous delights* (STC 16662), draws extensively upon *SC*. Thomas Nashe, in *Christs Teares Over Jerusalem* (STC 18366), refers to Harvey as 'this vaine *Braggadachio*'. Henry Peacham, *The Garden of Eloquence Conteining The Moste Excellent Ornaments, Exornations, Lightes, flowers, and formes of speech* (STC 19498), p. 15, referring to onomatopeia, writes: 'Touching this part I will refer the Reader to *Chaucer* & *Gower*, and to the new Shepherds calender, a most singular imitation of ancient speech.' George Peele, *The Honour of the Garter* (STC 19539), sig. A 4–A 4ᵛ, refers to *Hobbin*, Harvey in *SC*.

1594

S serves as Queen's Justice for County Cork in this year.

February

Lord Roche again complains that 'Edmund Spenser, of Kilcolman, gentleman, hath entered into three plough-lands, parcell of Ballingerath, and disseised your suppliant thereof, and continueth by countenaunce and greatnes the possession thereof, and maketh great waste of the wood of the said lands, and converteth a great deale of corne growinge thereupon to his proper use, to the damage of the complainant of two hundred pounds sterling. Whereunto the said Edmund Spenser, appearinge in person, had several dayes prefixed unto hime peremptorilie to answere, which he neglected to do. Therefore, after a daye of grace was given, on the 12th of February, 1594 [1595?], Lord Roche was decreed his possession.'

12   S having appeared in court, Lord Roche is decreed possession of disputed lands.

May

16   Sir William Russell appointed Lord Deputy of Ireland.

June

11   'St Barnabas' Day', S marries Elizabeth Boyle, kinswoman of Richard Boyle, later earl of Cork; one child, named Peregrine,

'Lat. Strange or outlandish', according to Camden, who includes it in a list of Christian names. (A second son by this marriage, Lawrence, is conjectured by a nineteenth-century Irish antiquary. A Lawrence Spenser resided at Bandon in Cork, and died in 1654. There has also been some speculation concerning another daughter, Margaret.) The courtship and marriage are recorded in *Amoretti* and *Epithalamion*.

November

19 S's *Amoretti* and *Epithalamion* entered in Stationers' Register, 'written not long since'. Dedicated to Sir Robert Needham by the publisher, William Ponsonby. In Sonnet 80 of *Amoretti* S reveals that he has completed the six books of *FQ*. It is possible that *FQ* IV–VI came over in the same ship as *Amor.* and *Epith.* with Needham.

December

13 Invitations to Revels at Gray's Inn sent out.
20 Beginning of Revels at Gray's Inn.

Publication of Richard Beacon's *Solon his follie*, Oxford. *Greenes Funeralls. By RB. Gent.*, sigs A 4 and B 2, contains references to Guyon and Colinet respectively. Richard Barnfield, *The Affectionate Shepheard* (STC 1480), sigs. E^v–E^{ij}, echoes *FQ* VI viiii 19ff. There is also a reference to *Col.* and *SC* on sig. E^{iij}. Samuel Daniel, *Delia and Rosamond augmented. Cleopatra* (STC 6254), sig. H 7, contains reference to S and Philip Sidney. Hadrian Dorrell, *to the gentle & courteous Reader*, prefixed to *Willobie his Auisa* (STC 25755), sig. A 2^v, refers to 'the dainetie Fayry Queene'. Michael Drayton, *Matilda. The faire and chaste Daughter of the Lord Robert Fitzwater* (STC 7205), sig. B 2^v, refers to 'Collin in thy Britomart'. Lewis Lewkenor, *The Resolved Gentleman*, translated from the French of Oliver de La Marche (STC 15139), p. 45, predicts: 'that the following ages among millions of other noble workes penned in her praise, shall as much admire the writer, but farre more the subject of the fairie Queene'. *The Masque of Proteus*, in Harleian MS 541, f. 145^a, echoes *FQ* I and its portrayal of Arthur, as Holiness, with his diamond shield. Thomas Nashe, *The Unfortunate Traveller. Or the life of Jacke Wilton* (STC 18380), sig. C, refers to 'goose-quill Braggadoches'. I. O., *The Lamentation of Troy, for the death of Hector. Whereunto is annexed an Olde womans Tale in hir solitarie Cell* (STC 18755), sigs A 3^v and B 2, praises S. *The First part of the Tragicall raigne of Selimus* (STC 12310ᵃ), contains numerous echoes of *FQ. Zepheria* (STC 26124), contains verbal echoes of S.

1595

January
3 Small masque of Amity at Gray's Inn Revels, whose audience includes: 'The Lord Keeper, the Earls of Shrewsbury, Cumberland, Northumberland, Southampton, and Essex, the Lords Buckhurst, Windsor, Mountjoy, Sheffield, Compton, Rich, Burleygh, Mounteagle, and the Lord Thomas Howard, Sir Thomas Heneage, Sir Robert Cecill; with a great number of Knights, Ladies, and very worshipful Personages.' The masque echoes *FQ* IV x 26–7.

March
2/3 Larger masque of Proteus at Gray's Inn Revels. Prepared by two poets and fellow members of Gray's Inn, Thomas Campion and Francis Davison, the masque appears to draw heavily on *FQ* IV xi and V ix. Davison's father, William, passed on the death warrant for Mary Queen of Scots, was defended by Lord Grey, and made a map of Ireland during his time in the Tower.

April
9 William Robinson appointed attorney general of Munster.

May
4 Arrival in Waterford of Sir John Norris as military commander for Ireland.

June
23 Earl of Tyrone proclaimed a traitor.

Publication of *Amoretti* and *Epithalamion* as a single volume. Publication of *Col.*, London. Dated from Kilcolman, 27 December 1591 and dedicated to Raleigh: 'this simple pastorall . . . agreeing with the truth in circumstance and matter' records Raleigh's visit to S's Cork estate, their voyage to England, and stay at court. The composite volume includes *Astrophel. A Pastorall Elegie upon the death of the most Noble and valorous Knight, Sir Philip Sidney,* and six other elegies on Sidney's death by Bryskett and others. Publication of *Am.* and *Epith.* Commendatory sonnet by S in William Jones's English translation of *Nennio, or a Treatise of Nobility.*

References to S in the following works: Richard Carew, *The Excellencie of the English tongue by R. C. of Anthony Esquire to W. C.,* in Camden's *Remains, concerning Britaine,* 1614 (STC 4522), p. 44, includes S. in list of English authors. Francis Bacon, 'The Speeches drawn up by Mr. Francis Bacon for the Earl of Essex in a device exhibited by his Lordship before Queen Elizabeth, on the anniversary of her accession to the throne, November 17, 1595', in *Letters, Speeches, Charges, Advices, &c of Francis Bacon . . . Now first published by Thomas Birch,* 1763, p. 14, contains echo of S: 'And as for you, untrue Politique, but truest bondman to *Philautia,* you, that presume to bind occasion, and to overwork fortune, I would ask you but one question.' Richard Barnfield, *Cynthia. With Certaine Sonnets, and the Legend of Cassandra* (STC 1483), *To the curteous Gentlemen Readers,* sig. A 4ᵛ, presents his work as 'the first imitation of the verse of that excellent Poet, Maister *Spencer,* in his *Fayrie Queene'.* E. C., *Emaricdulfe,* (STC 4268), sonnet 40, sig. C 7ᵛ, praises Elizabeth by allusion to S:

> Thy vertues *Collin* shall immortalize,
> *Collin* chast vertues organ sweetst esteem'd,
> When for *Elizas* name he did comprise
> Such matter as inventions wonder seem'd.

H. C., *Piers Plainness seaven yeres Prentiship,* Bodleian MS Malone 670, sig. C 2ᵛ, refers to '*Thrasilio* that base Braggadoche'. Thomas Campion, *Epigrammatum Liber,* in *Poemata* (STC 4544), sig. E 6ᵛ, contains this on S:

> *Ad. Ed. Spencerum.*
> Siue Canis siluas Spencere, vel horrida belli
> Fulmina, disperea ni te ame, & intime ame.

Thomas Churchyard, *A Musicall Consort of Heavenly harmonie (compounded out of many parts of Musicke) called Churchyards Charitie* (STC

5245), *To the Generall Readers*, sig. A 4, echoes *Col.* 396–9. In the same text, but with a separate title page (sig. E 3), Churchyard's *A praise of Poetrie, some notes thereof drawen out of the Apologie, the noble minded Knight, Sir Phillip Sidney wrate*, G 3ᵛ, declares:

> In Spenser morall fairie Queene
> And Daniels rosie mound
> If they be throwly waid and seen
> Much matter may be found.

Anthony Copley, *Wits Fittes and Fancies. Fronted and entermedled with Presidentes of Honour and Wisdome. Also Loves Owle: and idle conceited Dialogue between Love and an Olde-man* (STC 5739), *To the Gentlemen Readers*, sig. A 3, contains this apology: 'As for my *Loves Owle*, I am content that *Momus* turn it to a tennis-ball if he can, & bandy it quite away: namelie, I desire that M. *Daniel*, M. *Spencer*, & other the Prime Poets of our time, to pardon it with as easie a frowne as they please, for that I give them to understand, that an Universitie Muse never pend it, though humbly devoted thereunto.' William Covell, *Polimanteia . . . Whereunto is added England to Her Three Daughters, Cambridge, Oxford, Innes of Court, and to all the rest of her Inhabitants* (STC 5883), sig. Qᵛ, says of Cambridge: 'So onely without compare, eternallie should you live; for in your children shall the love-writing muse of divine *Sydnay*, and the pure flowing streame of Chrystallin *Spenser* survive onely: write then of *Elizas* raigne, a taske onely meete for so rare a pen'. There is a further compliment to S on sig. R 2ᵛ: 'Let divine *Bartasse* eternally praise worthie for his weeks worke, say the best thinges were made first: Let other countries (sweet Cambridge) envie, (yet admire) my *Virgil*, thy petrarch, divine *Spenser*.' Michael Drayton, *Endimion and Phoebe. Ideas Latmus* (STC 7192. *Works*, ed. J. W. Hebel, Oxford 1931–41), Hebel 1.153:

> Deare *Collin*, let my Muse excused be,
> Which rudely thus presumes to sing by thee,
> Although her straines be harsh untun'd & ill,
> Nor can attayne to thy divinest skill.

Thomas Edwards, *Cephalus and Procris. Narcissus* (STC 7525), sig. A 2ᵛ, 'The teares of the muses have bene teared from *Helicon*', a reference to *TM*. Edwards constantly praises S, for example:

> *Collyn* was a mighty swaine,
> In his power all do flourish,
> We are shepheards but in vaine,
> There is but one tooke the charge,
> By his toile we do nourish,
> And by him inlarg'd.

> He unlockt *Albions* glorie,
> He twas tolde of *Sidneys* honor,
> Onely he of our stories,
> Must be sung in greatest pride,
> In an Eglogue he hath wonne her,
> Fame and honor on his side.

Thomas Lodge, *A Fig for Momus: Containing Pleasant varietie, including Satyres, Eclogues, and Epistles* (STC 16658), Eglogue I, sig. B 4, is addressed *To reverend Colin*; W. S., *The Lamentable Tragedie of Locrine, the eldest sonne of King Brutus* (STC 21528), includes numerous borrowings from *Comp.*; Robert Southwell, *St. Peters Complaint* (STC 22956–7), *The Author to the Reader*, sig. A 3ᵛ, first line possibly suggested by *TM*: 'This makes my mourning muse resolve in teares.' Joshua Sylvester, *The Epistle Dedicatorie To . . . M. Anthonie Bacon*, prefacing Sylvester's translation, *The First Day of the Worldes Creation: Or Of the first weeke of that most Christian Poet, W. Salustius, Lord of Bartas* (STC 21658), sig. A 2: 'this most Christian Poet, and noble *Frenchman Lord of Bartas*, might have been naturalized amongst us, either by a generall act of a Poeticall Parliament: or have obtained a kingly translator for his weeke (as he did for his Furies:) or rather a divine *Sidney*, a stately *Spencer*, or a sweet *Daniell* for an interpreter thereof'.

1596

About this time, there are references to S in the following works: William Lisle, *To the Readers*, prefixed to his translation, *Part of Du Bartas, English and French, and in his Owne Kinde of Verse*, 1625 (STC 21663), sig. 4–4ᵛ, refers to metrical pattern of *FQ*; Henry Stanford, Presentation Verses in Cambridge University MS D.d.V.75, f. 16, recording a New Year's gift of 1595/6 or 1596/7:

In sign y^t thou art fair & matcheles w^{t}hout peere
I send this fayrie quene & wishe ye a new happie yeare
And all suche earthly joyes as hart can wishe or crave
and after long expense of yeres a seate in heaven to have.

January
13 A St John's College, Oxford, play by D. Rollinson entitled
Silvanus (Bodleian MS Douce 21808) is performed, with one of
the songs employing the metre and refrain of the roundelay in
SC Aug.
20 *FQ* books IV–VI entered in the Stationers' Register.

June
(Late) Raid on Spanish fleet moored at Cadiz by 2nd earl of Essex.

June–July
S believed to have completed bulk of *View* during these summer
months. Some critics believe Essex to be the unnamed dedicatee of
the *View*, and the 'one upon whom the eye of all England is fixed'.

September
 1 Spenser's *Fowre Hymnes* dedicated from the court at
Greenwich.
14 Essex writes to Antonio Perez, alluding to Ireland, at a time
when he was being considered for the Irish viceroyalty.

Sir Richard Bingham suspended pending royal inquiry on conduct
in Connaught.

October
15 Henry Gosnall succeeds William Robinson as attorney general
of Munster.

November
 1 Second part of *FQ* in circulation by this time. Robert Bowes,
the English secretary in Scotland, writes from Linlithgow to
Lord Burghley, conveying James VI's displeasure at *FQ* (*CSPS*
12.288): 'His Majesty has commanded me to certify you that so
many as are there of the second part of the "Ferry Queene" he
will not have sold here and further he will complain to Her

Majesty of the author as you will understand at more length by himself.'

8 S may have attended wedding of Earl of Worcester's daughters, celebrated in *Proth*.

12 Bowes writes to Burghley again outlining James's objections to the representation of his mother, Mary Queen of Scots, in *FQ* V ix (*CSPS* 12.291): 'The King has conceived great offence against Edward Spenser (Spencer) publishing in print in the second part of the "Fairy Queen" and 9th chapter som dishonourable effects (as the King deems thereof) against himself and his mother deceased. He alleged that this book was passed with privilege of Her Majesty's Commissioners for the view and allowance of all writings to be received into print. But therein I have (I think) satisfied him that it is not given out with such privilege. Yet he still desires that Edward Spenser for his fault may be duly tried and punished.'

Publication of *FQ* IV–VI. Publication of S's *Prothelamion*, spousal verse celebrating the betrothal of the two eldest daughters of the Earl of Worcester. Publication of *FQ* IV–VI together with second edition of *FQ* I–III. Publication of *Fowre Hymnes (Of Love, Of Beautie, Of Heavenly Love, Of Heavenly Beautie)*, the first two composed 'in the greener times of my youth'. This volume includes *Daphnaida*, second edition. Commendatory sonnet by S to de La Vardin, *History of George Castriot, surnamed Scanderbeg*, trans. by Zacharay Jones.

References to S in the following works: Thomas Churchyard, *A pleasant Discourse of Court and Wars . . . Written by Thomas Churchyard, and called his Cherishing (STC 5249)*, sig. B:

> The platform where all Poets thrive,
> Save one whose voice is hoarse they say.

Echoes *Col.* 396–9; Anthony Copley, *A Fig for Fortune (STC 5737)*, is a Roman Catholic adaptation of *FQ* I, directed against the Anglican Church; Sir John Davies, *Orchestra or A Poeme of Dauncing (STC 6360)*, shows influence of *HL*, and refers on st. 128, sig. C 8, to '*Colins* fayre heroike stile'; Charles Fitzgeffrey, *Sir Frances Drake (STC 10943)*, sig. B 5–B 5ᵛ, refers to 'SPENSER, whose hart inharbours *Homers* soule'; Bartholomew Griffin, *Fidessa, more chaste then kind (STC 12367)*, sig. E 4:

I tooke her to be beauties Queene alone,
But now I see she is a senseles stone.

See *Am.* 54. For the name *Fidessa*, see *FQ* I ii 26.2 and I iv 2.1–4; Sir John Harington, *A New Discourse of a Stale Subject, Called the Metamorphosis of Ajax* (*STC* 12779), sigs Aa^v–A[a] 2: 'They descanted of the new Faerie Queene and the old both, and the greatest fault they could finde in it was that the last verse disordered their mouthes, and was like a trycke of xvii. in a sinkapace.' On sig. Bb 5^v, Harington, addressing Sir John Spencer, 'a good substanciall free-holder in Northamptonshire', brother of Lady Elizabeth Carey, makes a further allusion to S: 'You have a learned Writer of your name, make much of him, for it is not the least honour of your honourable family'; Richard Linche, *Diella, Certaine Sonnets, adjoyned to the amorous Poeme of Dom Diego and Gineura. By R. L. Gentleman* (*STC* 17091), shows influence of Spenserian sonnet scheme and echoes of *Am.*; Thomas Lodge, *A Margarite of America* (*STC* 16660), sig. F 4, echoes *FQ* IV v 33ff.; Thomas Lodge, *Wits Miserie, and the Worlds Madnesse* (*STC* 16677), p. 57: 'SPENCER, best read in ancient Poetry'; Thomas Nashe, *Have With You to Saffron-Walden* (*STC* 18369). There are numerous references to S throughout Nashe's text. On sig. F 2, Nashe upbraids Gabriel Harvey: 'For having found by much shipwrackt experience, that no worke of his absolute under hys owne name, would passe, he used heretofore to drawe *Sir Philip Sydney, Master Spencer*, and other men of highest credit into everie pild pamphlet he set foorth'. On sig. R, Nashe adds S's name to a roll-call of influential intellectuals: 'as also in like sort Master *Spencer*, whom I do not thrust in the lowest place, because I make the lowest valuation of, but as wee use to set *Summ' tot'* alway underneath or at the bottome, he being the *Sum' tot'* of whatsoever can be said of sharpe invention and schollership'; William Smith, *Chloris* (*STC* 22872), with two dedicatory sonnets to S on sig. A 2, addressed to *To the Most Excellent and learned Shepheard Collin Clout*, and echoes of S in other sonnets; between now and 1600, a play is written entitled *I. T. Grim the Collier of Croyden; or, The Devil and his Dame: with the Devil and Saint Dunston*, first printed in *Gratiae Theatrales, or A Choice Ternary of English plays*, 1662. On sig. G 3 there begins a forty-seven-line version of the Malbecco-Hellenore episode in *FQ* III ix 10. The plot as a whole tells the same story.

1597

Sometime this year S purchases lands of Renny in south Cork, for £200, for his newborn son Peregrine, and acquires Buttevant Abbey. A draft book of Orders of the Revenue side of the Exchequer of 1609 contains the following entry: 'Corke, Edmonde Spencer, Kilvrogan, Kilwanton, Backbeliston, Neghwan, Ballintegan, Rynny, in Conte Corke, sp'ualities and temp'alities'.

March
5　Thomas, Lord Burgh, appointed Lord Deputy of Ireland. S completes *View* about now.

September
*c.*9　Death of Sir John Norris.
20　Sir Thomas Norris appointed president of Munster.

October
29　Earl of Ormond appointed military commander of Ireland. Thomas Norris appointed Justice of Ireland.

November
26　Archbishop Adam Loftus and Robert Gardiner appointed Justices of Ireland.

Publication of *SC*, fifth edition.
　References to S in the following works: Francis Beaumont, letter from Francis Beaumont to Thomas Speght, prefixed to Speght's edition of *The Workes of* . . . *Geffrey Chaucer*, 1598 (*STC* 5077–9), sig. A iii^v: 'But yet so pure were Chaucer's wordes in his owne daies, as *Lidgate* that learned man calleth him *The Loadstarre of the English language*; and so good they are in our daies, as Maister *Spencer*, following the counsaile of *Tullie in de Oratore*, for reviving of antient wordes, hath adorned his own stile with that beauty and gravitie, which *Tully* speaks of: and his much frequenting of *Chaucers* antient speeches causeth many to allow farre better of him, then otherwise they would'; Joseph Hall, *Virgidemiarum, Sixe Bookes. First three Bookes, Of Tooth-lesse Satyrs* (*STC* 12716), contains references to and echoes of *FQ* and *SC*; George Kirkbye, *The first set Of English Madrigalls to 4. 5. and 6. voyces* (*STC* 15010), sig. B ij^v, *SC Nov* 53–62 set to music; J. S., *Certaine Worthye Manuscript Poems of*

great Antiquitie Reserved long in the Studie of a Northfolke Gentleman.
And now first published by J. S. (STC 21499), verso of title-page, *To the*
worthiest Poet Maister Ed. Spenser; John Salisbury, poems included in
Robert Parry's *Sinetes Passions Uppon His Fortunes* (STC 19338),
Poesie XII. The authors muse upon his Conceyte, sig. E 7:

> Faire, fairest, faire: if passing faire, be faire,
> Let not your deed's obscure your beauties faire,
> The Queene so faire of Fearies not more fayer,
> Which doth excell with fancies chiefest fayer,
> Fayre to the worldes faire admiring wonder,
> Fayrer than Joves love that kills with thunder.

1598

February

7   S fails to pay arrearages of rent on the Abbey of Buttevant: '7
    mo Februar, 1597 [1598 n.s.], Mr. Spencer by Mr. Cheffe
    Barron's dirrecc'on under his hand hathe day ffor payment of
    the arreradgis of rent due uppon the Abbay of Buttevant untill
    the beginning of Easter terme next, ffor that at this present, by
    reasonn of trouble in the way, he durst not bring downe anie
    monny.' (This reference comes from Ferguson's 'Memorials'
    [see Bibliography]. Ferguson worked in the Irish Record Office
    in Dublin in the mid-nineteenth century. The entry is said to
    have come from a Book of Orders of the Revenues of the Irish
    Exchequer. These records were apparently destroyed by fire in
    1922, during the Irish Civil War.)

25 George Nicholson, a servant of Robert Bowes, writes to Sir
    Robert Cecil (*CSPS* 52.126) informing him that one Wal-
    ter Quin, an Irishman based at St Andrew's University, is
    'answering Spencer's book wherat the King was offended'.
    James VI had at the same time commissioned Robert Wal-
    grave, the royal printer, to publish a book by Quin asserting
    his claim to the English throne.

April

14 S's *View* entered in Stationers' Register: *A viewe of the present*
    state of Ireland. Discoursed by waye of a Dialogue betwene Eudoxus

and Irenius. Probably written 1592–6; circulating in manuscript but not published until 1633. One surviving copy – Bodleian MS Rawl. B. 478 – prepared for intended publication in 1598, has a note at the end from the Warden of the Stationers' Company to the Secretary: 'Mr Collinges/pray enter this Copie for mathew Lownes to be prynted when he do bringe other authoritie. Thomas Man.' This manuscript was collated in *Variorum*, and used by Renwick for his edition of 1934.

August
14   English forces routed at the Yellow Ford.

September
30   S nominated for post of sheriff of Cork by the privy council, including Robert Devereux, the second earl of Essex (BM Harleian MS 286, p. 272): 'A letter to the LSs Justices of of [*sic*] Ireland. Though we doubt not but yow will wthout any motio[n] from us have good regard for the appointing of meete and serviceable p[er]sons to bee sheriffs in the severall counties wch is a matter of great importance especially at this tyme when all p[ar]ts of the Realme are touched with the infection of Rebellion. Yet wee thinke it not amiss therefore to com[m]end unto you such men as wee hold to bee fitt for that office. Amonge whom wee may in fully [formally?] reckon Edmond Spencer a gentleman dwelling in the countie of Corke who is so well known unto yor LSs for his good and comendable p[ar]ts (beeing a man endowed wth good know-ledge in learning and not unskillful as wthout experience in the service of the warrs) as wee need not use many woords in his behalf. And therefore as wee are of opinion that yo^w will favor him for hymself and of yor owne accord so we do pray yo^w that this letter [abbr.] may increase his credits so farr forth with yo^w as that he may not fayle to bee appointed Sheriffe of the countie of Cork unless there by yo^w knowen some im-portant cause to the contrary. We arre p[er]suaded he will so behave himself in the place as yo^w shall have just cause to allowe of O^r comendation and his good service. And so. [Rest blotted].'

October
4   Sir Thomas Norris, James Goold and George Thornton,

writing to the Privy Council from Kilmallock, make mention of a 2,000-strong force of Irish rebels marching on Arlo. S's estate threatened.

5 Three thousand Irish rebels invade Limerick, led by John Fitz Thomas and Captain Tyrrell.

6 James Goold, writing from Kilmallock, informs Sir Robert Cecil that Hugh Cuffe has abandoned his seignory and that he 'knows none able to keep his seignory'. The rebels are encamped at Rathkeale.

7 Defection of Sir Thomas Norris and panic of English in Munster. Munster plantation overthrown by Irish as part of Tyrone's rebellion.

10 James Fitz Thomas Desmond is proclaimed earl of Desmond, known as the 'sugan' or straw-rope earl because of the tenuousness of his title.

11 Rebels march on Kilmallock. Retire from two to five miles on espying English forces.

12 Rebels move on Mallow.

13 Rebels enter counties of Kerry and Desmond.

15 About this time, Kilcolman is sacked and razed. S and his family are reputed to have escaped through an underground passage known as the Fox Hole, which led to caves north of the castle. (The passage was still extant in 1840, according to the Dublin Ordnance Survey Office.) S flees to Cork city and takes refuge there with his wife. Contemporary reports include 'A Note of the spoils committed and of the towns burned, in the barony of Buttevant, by Onie O'More, James Fitz Thomas, Captain Tyrrell, and their associates, the 15th of October 1598' (*CSPI* 202.113).

16 The so-called earl of Desmond and his followers march on Lord Roche's land, killing and burning. Arthur Hyde's castle is assaulted, but the rebels are repulsed.

17 Sir Thomas Norris is ensconced in Cork.

20 Ormond, based at Youghal, makes a list of those undertakers who have abandoned their estates. The list includes major Munster landowners such as Raleigh, but not S.

21 The home of fellow undertaker Arthur Hyde is assaulted. Ormond writes to the Privy Council from Youghal (*CSPI* 202.117): 'I may not omit to acquaint your lordships that, at my coming into this Province, I found that the greatest part of the undertakers had most shamefully quitted and forsaken their

castles and houses of strength before even the traitors came near them, leaving all their spoils, whereby they furnished themselves with the arms and other munition that before served against them, to Her Majesty's dishonour, and the increasing of the traitors' pride. A note of many of them that were so forsaken and lost I do here-inclosed send you [see entry above], having given direction to the Lord President to see forthcoming the chiefest of them that so quitted their castles, to answer the same.'

23   Thomas Norris writes to Cecil from Cork, noting that John Barry, brother of Lord Barry, and David Roche, son of Lord Roche, both relatives of S's neighbours, are out in open rebellion.

22   Hyde's castle is overthrown and rifled of all contents.

26   William Saxey, Chief Justice of Munster, gives account of Tyrone's massacres in the province (*CSPI* 202.127). He includes amongst the 'causes that have begotten this calamity': 'The slackness of the undertakers in not peopling of their seignories with English inhabitants hath wrought such weak means of defence against traitors and rebels, as the English are not able (in this or like tumult) to help one another.'

28   Arthur Hyde, one of the dispossessed undertakers, informs the Privy Council that Lord Barry, S's neighbour, helped Hyde's wife and children to escape to Cork. Raleigh, as Lieutenant of Cornwall, acts as military adviser in the sending of 2,000 English soldiers to Munster.

A discourse by one William Weever written about this time (*CSPI* 202.138) describes the events of the Munster Rebellion, and notes that: 'Only one English gentleman, who inhabited in those deserts (whose name he knoweth not), having an Irish priest with him, escaped in this manner. The priest saluted the new Earl, and said that the said gentleman and his family were Catholics, so as the Earl made proclamation that no man should do them any harm, and thus, being spoiled of all their goods, they passed with their lives and apparel to Cork.' This English gentleman may have been S.

November
At the end of this month 2,000 English soldiers bound for Cork land at Waterford.

December

5 The Privy Council is informed that the sheriff of Cork and the majority of the Undertakers, together with their families, were ensconsed in Cork at the outbreak of the Munster Rebellion.

7 S, sheriff of Cork, reported to be in Cork: 'Captains Thos. Southwell and Timothy Cottrell to the Privy Council (*CSPI* 202, pt 4.12): 'The Lord President, the Bishops of Cork and Down, the Provost Marshal, and the sheriff of the County of Cork with the most part of the undertakers, their wives and children, placed in Cork at the beginning of the rebellion. There they yet remain, besides a number of Welshmen and other distressed poor people, relieved by the citizens to their uttermost.'

9 S leaves Cork, with instructions to deliver a letter written by Sir Thomas Norris, President of Munster, to the Privy Council (*CSPI* 202.15): 'Sir Thomas Norreys to the Privy Council . . . [there follows a detailed description of the military situation in Munster wherein Norris gives thanks for the arrival of reinforcements from England]. This despatched by the hand of Edmund Spenser, the poet.'

21 Sir Thomas Norris writes to the Privy Council once more from Cork (*CSPI* 202.36): 'It may please your honourable Lordships. Since my last of the 9th of this month, and (*sic*) sent by Mr. Spenser &c.'

24 S probably at Whitehall with letter from Norris. S delivers own views on behalf of dispossessed planters: *A briefe note of Ireland*, which includes an address to the Queen and 'Certaine pointes to be considered of in the recovering of the Realme of Irelande'. See *PRO*, SP 63/202 pt 4/59, for copy in the hand of Sir Dudley Carleton (1573–1632), inscribed in a later hand 'A briefe discourse of Ireland, by Spenser'. First published, from this manuscript, in *The Complete Works of Spenser*, ed. A. B. Grosart (London 1882–4) vol. I, pp. 537–55: Printed from this manuscript in *Variorum*. Some critics believe only the last section of the *briefe note*, 'Certaine pointes', is exclusively by S.

29 Norris's second letter, dated 21 December, received at Whitehall.

30 S paid sum of £8 for carrying letters from Norris to Privy Council: 'To Edwarde Spencer gent uppon a warr^t. signed by Mr. Secretarie dated at Whitehall xxx^{mo} Decembris 1598 for bringing lres. for her ma^{te} speciall service from Sir Thomas

Norrys Lo: President of Mounster viii. li' (*PRO* E. 351/543, f. 40ʳ). This suggests that Ben Jonson's claim that S died 'for lack of bread' is unfounded.

Publication of Sidney's collected works by William Ponsonby.
References to S in the following works: Richard Barnfield, *Poems: In divers humors* (STC 1488), sonnet I, *To his friend Maister R. L. In praise of Musique and Poetrie*, sig. E 2:

> *Dowland* to thee is deare; whose heavenly tuch
> Upon the Lute, doeth ravish humaine sense:
> *Spenser* to mee; whose deepe Conceit is such,
> As passing all Conceit, needs no defence.

Barnfield praises S again in *A Remembrance of some English Poets*, sig. E 2ᵛ:

> Live *Spenser* ever, in thy *Fairy Queene*:
> Whose like (for deepe Conceit) was never seene.
> Crownd mayst thou bee, unto thy more renowne,
> (As King of Poets) with a Lawrell crowne.

And in *An Ode*, sig. E 2ᵛ, Barnfield echoes *FQ* II vi 24; Samuel Brandon, *The Tragicomoedi of the vertuous Octavia* (STC 3544), act 2, scene 1, sigs C 4ᵛ–C 5, echoes *FQ* VII vii; Charles Butler, *Rhetoricae Libri Duo* (STC 4197), sigs C 3ᵛ–C 4, quotes *RT* 400–6, and includes S in a list of famous poets; Richard Carew (?), *A Herrings Tayle* (STC 4614), sig. B 4ᵛ:

> But neither can I tell, ne can I stay to tell,
> This pallace architecture, where perfections dwell:
> Who list such know, let him *Muses despencier* reede,
> Or thee, whom *England* sole did since the conquest
>   breed,
> To conquer ignorance, *Sidney* like whom endite,
> Even *Plato* would, or *Jove* (they say) like Plato write.

George Chapman, *The Blinde Beggar of Alexandria* (STC 4965), sig. B

3: 'Br. I am signeor Braggadino the Martiall spaniardo the aide of AEgypt in her present wars'; Edward Guilpin, Skialetheia, Or, A shadowe of Truth, in certaine Epigrams and Satyres (STC 12504), Satyra sexta, sig. E:

> Some blame deep Spencer for his grandam words,
> Others protest that, in them he records
> His maister-peece of cunning giving praise,
> And gravity to his profound-prickt layes.

Giovanni Paolo Lomazzo, A Tracte Containing the Artes of curious Paintinge (STC 16698), contains marginal notes by 'R[ichard] H[aydocke] student in Physik', the English translator of Lomazzo, supporting the analogies made between painting and poetry, for example, p. 85: 'Our English Painters may reade Sir Ph: Sidney, Spencer, Daniel, &c.' There is also an allusion to FQ on p. 51; John Marston, The Scourge of Villainy (STC 17485), satire 6, Hem nosti'n, sig. E 7:

> Another yet dares tremblingly come out,
> But first he must invoke good Colyn Clout.

And on sig. E 7ᵛ, Marston continues:

> Here's one, to get an undeserv'd repute
> Of deepe deepe learning, all in fustian sute
> Of ill-plac'd farre-fetch'd words attiereth
> His period, that sence forsweareth.
>
> Another makes old Homer, Spencer cite
> Like my Pygmalion, where, with rare delight
> He cryes, O Ovid . . .

Francis Meres, Palladis Tamia. Wits Treasury. Being the Second part of Wits Common wealth (STC 17834), makes several references to S. On f. 278ᵛ: 'And our famous English Poet Spenser, who in his Sheepeheards Calender lamenting the decay of Poetry at these dayes, saith most sweetly to the same.

> The make thee wings of thine aspiring wit
> And whence thou camest fly back to heaven apace, &c.

On f. 280ᵛ:

As Sextius Propertius saide; *Nescio quid magis nascitur Iliade*: so I say of *Spencers Fairy Queene*, I knowe not what more excellent or exquisite Poem may be written.

As *Achilles* had the advantage of *Hector*, because it was his fortune to be extolled and renowned by the heavenly verse of *Homer*: so *Spensers Elisa* the *Fairy Queen* hath the advantage of all the Queenes in the worlde, to bee eternized by so divine a Poet.

As *Theocritus* is famoused for his *Idyllia* in *Greeke*, and *Virgill* for his *Eclogs* in Latine: so *Spencer* their imitatour in his *Shepheardes Calender*, is renowned for the like argument, and honoured for fine Poeticall invention, and most exquisite wit.

On ff. 282ᵛ–283:

As *Homer* and *Virgil* among the Greeks and Latines are the chiefe Heroick Poets: so *Spencer* and *Warner* be our chiefe heroicall Makers.

As *Pindarus*, *Anacreon* and *Callimachus* among the Greekes; and *Horace* and *Catallus* among the Latines are the best Lyrick Poets: so in this faculty the best amon[n]g our Poets are *Spencer* (who excelleth in all kinds) *Daniell, Drayton, Shakespeare, Bretton*.

William Rankins, *Seaven Satyres Applyed to the weeke* (STC 20700), *Induction*, sig. A 3ᵛ, echoes *FQ* II iii 4ff.:

Of Love, of Courtships and of fancies force
Some gilded Braggadachio may discourse:
My shaggy Satyres doe forsake the woods, . . .
To view the manner of this humane strife.

Thomas Rogers, *Celestiall Elegies of the Goddesses and the Muses, deploring the death of . . . the Ladie Fraunces Countesse of Hertford* (STC 21225), shows influence of *TM*; Francis Rous, *Thule, Or Vertues Historie. To the Honorable and vertuous Mistris Amy Avdeley. By F. R.* (STC 21348), uses characters and episodes adapted from *FQ*;

Thomas Speght, *The Workes of our Antient and Learned English Poet, Geffrey Chaucer, newly Printed (STC 5077–9)*, sig. Ciii–Ciii^v:

And as for men of later time, not onely that learned gentle-man M. William Thynne, in his Epistle Dedicatorie to the Kings Majestie, but also two of the purest and best writers of our daies: the one for Prose, the other for Verse, M. *Ascham* and M. *Spenser*, have delivered most worthy testimonies of their approoving of him. . . .

Master *Spenser* in his first Eglogue of his Shepheardes Kalender, calleth him *Titirus*, the god of Shepheardes, com-paring him to the worthinesse of the Roman Titirus Virgil. In his Faerie Queene in his discourse of friendship, as thinking himselfe most worthy to be Chaucers friend, for his like naturall disposition that Chaucer had, hee sheweth that none that lived with him, nor none that came after him, durst presume to revive Chaucers lost labours in that unperfite tale of the Squire, but only himselfe: which he had not done, had he not felt (as he saith) the infusion of Chaucers owne sweete spirite, surviving within him. And a little before he termeth him, Most renowned and Heroicall Poet: and his Writings, The workes of heavenly wit: concluding his com-mendation in this manner:

Dan Chaucer, Well of English undefiled,
On Fames eternal beadrole worthy to be filed.
I follow here the footing of thy feet,
That with thy meaning so I may the rather meet.

Robert Tofte, *Certain Divine Poems, written by the foresaid Author R. T. Gentleman*, appended to *Alba. The Months Minde of a Melancholy Lover (STC 24096)*, shows general influence of S's *Hymnes*; William Vaughan, *Poetum libellus (STC 24620)*, *Invitatur candidati Poete ad triumphales cantus . . . Roberti Comitis Essexij*, sig. A 4^v:

Huc Spencere veni qui vena praeditus alta
Virgilij plena pragmata voce canis.
Non lamijs Libitina tuis continget acerba
In mare dum Thamesis nobilis unda fluat.

1599

January

13 S dies at Westminster. Jonson told Drummond 'that the Irish having robbed Spenser's goods and burnt his house and a little child new born, he and his wife escaped, and after he died for lack of bread in King Street'.

16 S buried in Westminster Abbey at charge of earl of Essex. Jonson's assertion that S died 'for lack of bread', though supported by Camden, does not quite square with the £8 he was paid on 30 December 1598 and the fact that a pension of £25 was due at Christmas. S was buried, Camden records, 'near to Chaucer, at the charge of the Earl of Essex, his hearse being attended by poets, and mournful elegies and poems, with the pens that wrote them, thrown into the tomb'. Royal instruction to erect a memorial not implemented. Memorial finally erected in Westminster Abbey in 1620 by Ann Clifford, Countess of Dorset. The inscription read: 'Here lyes, expecting the second comminge of our Saviour Christ Jesus, the body of Edmond Spenser, the Prince of Poets in his tyme, whose divine spirit needs noe other witnesse than the workes which he left behind him.'

17 John Chamberlain, in a letter to Dudley Carleton (*SP Dom.*, Eliz. 270.16), writes: 'The Lady Cope your cousen and mine old mistress left the world (as I heare) on Tw'elvth Even and Spencer our principall poet coming out of Ireland died at Westminster on Satterday last.'

24 Sir Thomas Norris writes from Cork to Sir Robert Cecil, apparently unaware of S's death (*CSPI* 203.24): 'Since my last by Mr. Spenser, here hath happened so little matter, as I hold it not fit to trouble your Honour therewith.'

February

Nicholas Curtis, through Norris, complains to Sir Robert Cecil of his maltreatment at hands of Lodowick Bryskett since death of S (*CSPI* 203.61): 'The request of the President of Munster by his letter is, that it would please his Honour to protect Curteys against wrong and injury. Has served long in Ireland, "in that poor and troublesome place of Clerk of the Council in Munster", and held his state therein "upon the trust of Lodowick Bryskett and Edmund Spenser (men not unknown to your Honour)". Was for the same drawn to such conditions as took up his whole estate in England, which was then of good value. "Now, by this rebellion I have had all burned, and taken from me. The said Lodowick Bryskett, to press me down to the lowest degree of misery (Edmund Spenser being lately deceased, the mean and witness of our mutual trust and confidence), goeth about to take away the said place also; which if he be suffered to do by reason of my weakness and hard fortune, I having framed myself wholly, and those poor parts God hath given me, unto that service, I shall remain the most distressed man that liveth".'

March
12   S's last patron, Robert Devereux, earl of Essex, appointed Lord Lieutenant of Ireland.

Commendatory sonnet by S published in Gasper Contareno, *The Commonwealth and Government of Venice*, trans. L. Lewkenor.
    References to S in the following works: Hugh Holland, *On Spencer ye Poett* (BM Add. MS 21433, f. 177ᵛ):

> On Spencer yᵉ Poett.
> H H
> He was & is, see then where lyes the odds
> Once God of Poetts, now Poet of the Gods
> And though his lyne of life begone aboute
> Yᵉ life yet of his lyne shall never out.

Thomas Cutwode, *Caltha Poetarum: or The Bumble Bee* (STC 6151), sigs A 4ᵛ–A 5: 'For *Homer*, who imitated none, and *Archilocus*, who is compared with the curious Ape of *Homer*, because they only finished their workes in their life. And *Virgil*, the curious Ape of *Homer*. *Ovid* the Amorous, *Martiall* the lycentious, *Horace*, the mixt betwixt modest & *Satirique* vaine. The flower of our age, sweete pleasing *Sidney*. *Tasso* the grave. Pollished *Daniell* the Historick *Spencer* the Truthes Faith'; Samuel Daniel, *The Poeticall Essayes of Sam. Danyel* (STC 6261), *Musophilus: Containing a generall defence of all learning*, sig. C 4ᵛ:

> How many thousands never heard the name
> Of *Sydney*, or of *Spencer*, or their bookes?
> And yet brave fellowes, and presume of fame

And seem to beare downe all the world with lookes:
What then shall they expect of meaner frame,
On whose indevours few or none scarse looks?

Sir John Davies, *Nosce Teipsum* (STC 6355), contains echoes of
several works by S, including *FQ, HB* and *HL*; Anthony Gibson, *A
Woomans Woorth, defended against all the men in the world* (STC
11831), *To the Honourable Mistresse Margaret Ratcliffe*, f. A 7:

> Had I a *Spencers* spirit, a *Daniels* powers:
> Th'extracted quintessence were only yours.

Robert Greene (d.1592), *The Comicall Historie of Alphonsus King of
Aragon* (STC 12233), act I, sig. A 3ᵛ, echoes *FQ* I, proem 1:

> I which was wont to follow *Cupids* games
> Will put in ure *Minervaes* sacred Art,
> And this my hand which used for to pen
> The praise of love, and *Cupids* peerles power,
> Will now begin to treat of bloudie *Mars*,
> Of doughtie deeds and valiant victories.

Joseph Hall, *Virgidemiarum The three last Bookes. Of byting Satyres*
(STC 12719), lib. 4, sat. 1, p. 5, draws on *FQ* V i 12:

> Gird but the *Cynicks* Helmet on his head,
> Cares he for *Talus* or his flayle of lead?.

John Hoskins, *Direccons for Speech and Style*, BM MS Harleian 4604,
f. 6: 'Let Spencer tell yoᵂ such a tale of a *ffaery Queene*, & *Ovid* of
Diana & then it is a poets tale'; George Peele, *The Love of King David
and Fair Bethsabe* (STC 19540), sig. Eᵛ, echoes *FQ* I v 2:

> *Joab.* Beauteous and bright is he among the Tribes,
> As when the sunne attir'd in glist'ring robe,
> Comes dauncing from his orientall gate,
> And bridegroome-like hurles through the gloomy aire
> His radiant beames, such doth King David shew,
> Crownd with the honour of his enemies towne,
> Shining in riches like the firmament,

The starrie vault that overhangs the earth,
So looketh David King of Israel.

The First Booke of the Preservation of King Henry vii when he was but Earle of Richmond (STC 13076), sig. A 2ᵛ: 'I confesse and acknowledge that we have many excellent and singular good Poets in this our age, as Maister *Spencer*, that was, Maister *Gowlding*, Doctor *Phayer*, Maister *Harrington, Daniell*, and divers others whom I reverence in that kinde of prose-rhythme: wherein *Spencer* (with offence spoken) hath surpassed them all'; Robert Roche, *Eustathia or the Constancie of Susanna* (STC 21137), *To the Reader*, sig. A 3ᵛ:

Expect not heere, th'invention, or the vaine,
Of *Lucrece rape-write*: or the curious scan,
Of *Phillis* friend; or famous fairy-*Swaine*;
Or *Delias* prophet, or admired man.
My chicken faethered winges, no ympes enrich,
Pens not full fum'd, mount not so high a pitch.

Let *Colin* reare his flight to admiration
And traine his lovely flocke, his pipe to follow.
Let *Damons* reache, out-reach all imitation;
And frame melodious hymnes, to please *Apollo*.
The swaine that pend this pastorall for *Pan*
Thought once to end his worke, ere began.

John Weever, *Epigrammes in the oldest cut, and newest fashion* (STC 25223), *Lectores, quotquot, quales, quicunq; estis*, sigs A 5ᵛ–A 6:

Nor have I spent in *Troinovant* my dayes,
Where all good witts (some say) are crown'd with Bayes . . .
I never durst presume take in my hand
The nimble-tripping Faeries history,
I cannot, I protest, yet understand
The wittie, learned, Satyres mystery;
I cannot move the savage with delight,
Of what I cannot, Reader then I write

The first weeke, sig. B 1ᵛ:

Epig. 3. In Elizabetham.

If that *Elizium* be no fained thing,
Whereof the Poets wont so much to sing;
Then are those faire fields in this Faerie land,
Which faire *Eliza* rules with awful hand.

The fifth weeke, sig. F, draws on *FQ,* esp. *FQ* II ii 2.8–9 for the last
two lines:

Epig. 7. In Braggadochionem.
Did *Braggadochio* meete a man in field?
Tis true, he did, the way he could not shun:
And did he force great *Brundon* weapons yeeld;
Nay there he lies. To untrusse when he begun,
He stole his weapons and away did run:
Vaine is thy vaunt, and victorie unjust,
thou durst not stay till he his points untrust.

The sixt weeke, sig. F 8:

Epig. 23. In obitum Ed. Spencer Poetae prestantiss.
Colin's gone home, the glorie of his clime,
The Muses Mirrour, and the Shepheards Saint;
Spencer is ruin'd, of our latter time
The fairest ruine, Faeries foulest want:
When his *Time ruines* did our ruine show,
Which by his ruine we untimely know:
Spencer therfore thy *Ruines* were cal'd in,
Too soone to sorrow least we should begin.

The Spenser Circle

It is normal practice to see Spenser as part of a 'Circle' –
specifically the Leicester–Sidney Circle – rather than as the centre
of his own. Yet Spenser was a prominent official in Ireland long
after the deaths of these two early guardians. In compiling this
mass biography I have tried to include all of Spenser's major
literary influences, key contemporaries, fellow students, patrons,
acquaintances, admirers, Irish administrators, planters, as well as
his family. All of the Munster undertakers are named, as are all of
the recipients of the dedicatory sonnets to *The Faerie Queene*, and
the guests at Bryskett's house in Dublin.

Andrewes, Lancelot (1555–1626), bishop of Winchester, educated
at same institutions as Spenser, though not at precisely the same
time, first at Merchant Taylors' School, and then at Pembroke Hall,
Cambridge. Became a Fellow of both Pembroke Hall, and Jesus
College, Oxford. Took holy orders in 1580, and served as chaplain
to the earl of Huntingdon. He secured a living at St Giles's,
Cripplegate, in 1589, and was subsequently made prebendary of St
Paul's, and master of Pembroke until 1605.

Beacon, Richard (? –1611), Suffolk-born, Oxford-educated Irish
administrator and author. Entered St John's College on 12
November 1567, taking his BA in 1571 and his MA in 1575.
Admitted to Gray's Inn on 19 June 1577, he was called to the bar
on 27 January 1585. On 17 December 1586 he was appointed 'her
majesty's attorney for the province of Munster', at an annual
salary of £17, regulating crown grants. Beacon himself was granted
land in Cork and Waterford. Author of *Solon his follie* (1594), an
allegorical work drawing an analogy between Athens and Sala-
mina and England and Ireland. Close parallels with S in terms
both of career and literary interests.

Boyle, Elizabeth (?1576–1622), daughter of Stephen and Joan Boyle
of Bradden, Northamptonshire, not far from Althorp. She and one
of her brothers moved to Ireland probably because her kinsman
Richard Boyle, later first earl of Cork, was active in the viceregal

administration. Second wife of S, praised in *Epith.* She married S in 1594. They had one son, named Peregrine.

Bryskett, Lodowick (*c.*1546–1612), poet, translator, and Irish official. Cambridge educated. Served as Clerk of the Council in Ireland under Sidney in 1571. Became close friend of Sidney's son, Philip. In 1577 he became Clerk of the Chancery for the Faculties in Ireland, an office in which he was succeeded by S. In 1582, Lord Grey made him Secretary of the Munster Council. In *A Discourse of Civill Life,* dedicated to Lord Grey, Bryskett employs as a framing device the pretext of a gathering at his Dublin residence at which S was present. Bryskett contributed two elegies on Philip Sidney to those collected by S and published at the end of *Col.* Bryskett is represented by Thestylis in *Col.* S's sonnet number 33 in *Amor.* and *Epith.* is addressed to Bryskett.

Buchanan, George (1506–82), Scottish historian, scholar and translator, born at Killearn in Stirlingshire, studied in Paris and at St Andrew's, where he took his BA in 1526. Returned to Paris in 1528, and taught there for ten years. Returned to Scotland in 1537. Professor at Bordeaux from 1539 to 1542, where he had Montaigne as a pupil, then travelled to Portugal. Back in Paris by 1553, and in Scotland in 1561. Became Principal of St Leonard's College, St Andrew's in 1566, and Moderator of the General Assembly in 1567. Subsequently made Keeper of the Privy Seal and tutor to the young King James. Author of *De Jure Regni Apud Scotos,* written in 1567 to justify the deposition of Mary, but not published till 1579. His translation of Psalms into Latin brought him wide renown as a Latinist. His *History of Scotland,* in Latin, was published at Edinburgh, 1582. An associate of the Leicester–Sidney circle, Buchanan was singled out by Spenser in the *View* as his chief intellectual influence.

Butler, Thomas, 10th earl of Ormond (1532–1614), educated with Prince Edward at court. Succeeded to earldom in 1546. Returned to Ireland in 1544. Made a Privy Councillor in 1556. Made Lord Treasurer of Ireland in 1559. Led government forces against the earl of Desmond in the first stages of the Desmond Rebellion, 1579–81. Served as Governor of Munster in 1583, and again in 1594–6. Addressee of dedicatory sonnet accompanying first three books of *The Faerie Queene* in 1590. Ormond, a friend of Burghley and a favourite of the Queen, had been an opponent of the Leicester–Sidney faction at court, and Spenser's sonnet may be seen as a conciliatory move.

Bynneman, Henry (d. 1583), printer, made liveryman of the Stationers' Company on 30 June 1578. Archbishop Parker patronised him, allowing him to open a shed at the north west door of St Paul's. Parker asked Burghley to permit Bynneman to print 'a few usual Latin books for the use of grammarians, as Terence, Virgil, Tulley's offices, &c., a thing not done here in England before or very rarely'. Bynneman published the first edition of Holinshed's *Chronicles*, George Turberville's *Booke of Falconrie* and *Noble Art of Venerie* (both 1575), George Gascoigne's *Poems* (1575–6), and Harvey's Latin works (1577–8). He published the Spenser–Harvey correspondence in 1580, and Richard Stanyhurst's translation of the first four books of Virgil's *Aeneis* in 1583.

Campion, Edmund (1540–81), born in London on 25 January 1540, Edmund Campion entered St John's College, Oxford, on its foundation in 1557. He was junior proctor of that institution from April 1568 to April 1569. By August 1570, he had departed for Dublin amid an atmosphere of growing suspicion and religious persecution. During his stay in Dublin, Campion resided with the Stanyhursts. He was interested in a scheme then being put forward by Henry Sidney to establish a university in Dublin. From Ireland, Campion moved to the English college at Douay, where he renounced protestantism. He returned to England in 1580, and was arrested at Dover on 25 June. Released after a brief period of detention, he made his way to London to preach counter-reformation Catholicism, and may have sheltered at Leicester House while Spenser was there. Died a Jesuit martyr at Tyburn on 1 December 1581. Campion's *Two Bokes of the Histories of Ireland* was composed in Dublin between 1570 and 1571. The dedication, to Robert Dudley, then Chancellor of the University of which Campion was still a registered fellow, is dated from Dublin 27 May 1571.

Carew, George, 1st Baron of Clopton and 1st earl of Totnes (1555–1629), English soldier and administrator, friend of Walter Raleigh and authority on Irish affairs. Educated at Oxford, fought in the Irish wars of 1575–83. Punctuated his early years in Ireland with a voyage in the company of Sir Humphrey Gilbert. As lieutenant-general of English ordnance he accompanied the earl of Essex on the Cadiz expedition of 1596 and the voyage to the Azores in 1597. Served as President of Munster from 1600 to 1603.

Carey, Elizabeth, Lady Carew (d. 1618), one of the daughters of John Spencer of Althorp, and thus related to Spenser. A poet and translator of Petrarch, dedicatee of *Muiopotmos* and *The Faerie Queene*, wife of Sir George Carew. Praised as Charillis in *Colin Clouts Come Home Againe*.

Carey, Sir Henry, 1st Lord Hunsdon (c.1526–96), Lord Chamberlain and Governor of Berwick. A cousin and intimate of Elizabeth. Quelled the northern uprising in 1570. Dedicatee of *The Faerie Queene*.

Carleill, Christopher (c.1551–93), the son of a London vintner, has a typical New English pedigree. He was educated at Cambridge in the 1560s. In the 1570s, he saw active service in the Low Countries. As the son-in-law of Sir Francis Walsingham, he participated in the early 1580s in English efforts to colonise America. He was the author, in 1583, of *A discourse upon the entended voyage to the hethermoste partes of America*, which is to be found in Hakluyt's *The principal navigations, voyages, traffiques & discoveries of the English nation*. In 1584 he was appointed supreme commander of the garrison at Coleraine. He lost this post the following year, seemingly due to a disagreement with Perrot. In July 1588, he was installed as constable of Carrickfergus in Antrim. Present at Bryskett's house in Dublin when Spenser is said to have read from *The Faerie Queene*.

Cartwright, Thomas (1535–1603), radical protestant cleric, was nominated by Adam Loftus in 1567 for the bishopric of Armagh, which Loftus was then vacating to assume his duties as primate of all Ireland.

Cecil, William, Lord Burghley (1520–98), Elizabeth's Lord Treasurer, and English Secretary of State from 1550. Relations with Spenser strained because of suspicion of satire against Burghley in

Mother Hubbards Tale. Addressee of dedicatory sonnet prefacing 1590 edition of *The Faerie Queene*.

Chichester, Sir Arthur, Baron Chichester of Belfast (1563–1625), entered Exeter College, Oxford, in 1583, and had to flee to Ireland after assaulting a royal purveyor. Pardon granted by Elizabeth, after which he served against the Armada in 1588, in Drake's expedition of 1595, and in Cadiz with Essex in 1596. He was in France and the Low Countries in 1597, knighted the same year, and appointed Colonel of the regiment at Drogheda in 1598. He served in Ireland as governor of Carrickfergus during the Tyrone Rebellion (1599–1603), as Lord Deputy from 1604 to 1614, and Lord Treasurer from 1616 to 1625.

Churchyard, Thomas (?1520-1604), English-born soldier and literary adventurer, author of numerous pamphlets, best remembered for the poem 'Shore's Wife' in the *Mirror for Magistrates* (1563). He served as a soldier in Scotland and the Low Countries, and was with the first earl of Essex in Ireland in the early 1570s and later during the Desmond Rebellion of 1579-83. He served under Lord Grey both in Scotland and Ireland. In *Colin Clouts Come Home Againe* Spenser alludes to Churchyard as:

> old *Palemon* free from spight,
> Whose carefull pipe may make the hearer rew
> Yet he himselfe may rewed be more right,
> That hung so long untill quite hoarse he grew.

Churchyard refers to this notice in *A Musicall Consort* (1595) and *A Pleasant Discourse of Court and Wars* (1596). In *Churchyard's Challenge* (1593), he refers to Spenser as 'now the spirit of learned speech'.

Clifford, George, 3rd earl of Cumberland (1558–1605), naval commander, dedicatee of *The Faerie Queene*. A chivalric figure, he became Elizabeth's official Champion in 1590, representing her at the tilt.

Croft, Sir James (d. 1590), Lord Deputy of Ireland and Controller of Queen Elizabeth's Household. Knighted in 1547, and made governor of Haddington in 1549. Served in Calais in 1550. Moving to Ireland, he subdued Cork in 1551 but failed to pacify Connaught and Ulster. He was fined £500 in 1555 for being implicated in Wyatt's rebellion. In 1559 he was appointed governor of Berwick. He was made a privy councillor in 1570, and served on the commission for the trial of Mary Queen of Scots in 1586. Sir William Herbert, a prominent Munster undertaker, dedicated his Latin discourse on Ireland to Croft.

Dawtrey, Nicholas, another of the guests at Bryskett's house in Dublin, he arrived in Ireland in the 1560s, but he first appears in crown documents in September 1581, where he is reported as commander of a company of one hundred horse in Clandeboye, in east Ulster. Four years later we hear of him being despatched to the Scottish court on official business. He shared Carleil's disaffection with Perrot, as indeed did Spenser, and he did not resume his Irish commission. In 1588 he acted as Sergeant Major General of the queen's troops at Tilbury. Throughout the 'crisis' years of the 1590s, he contributed a series of position papers on Ireland to the government in the hope of once more attaining office there. He died in his 'adopted country' in 1601. Dawtrey was the subject of a curious piece of antiquarian excavation by one of his descendants in the 1920s, who claimed that his ancestor was a role-model for Shakespeare's Falstaff.

Derricke, John (fl. 1578), may have been a customs officer at Drogheda, or the 'Master Derrick', a surgeon, who served Sir Robert Sidney in the Low Countries from 1597 to 1601. Devised in 1578, Derricke's *Image of Irelande* (1581) was one of the most influential Elizabethan books on Ireland. The dedication to Philip Sidney is dated from Dublin 16 June 1578. One group of woodcuts are in the form of a 'strip cartoon', recording the downfall of Rory Og O'More at the hands of Sir Henry Sidney. With its twelve intricate woodcuts, its attacks on Catholicism, its dedication to Philip Sidney, its blend of classical mythology and contemporary satire, and its exultation of militant Protestantism, *The Image of Irelande* suggests itself as a text to be read alongside *The Shepheardes Calender*.

Devereux, Robert, 2nd earl of Essex (1567-1601), son of Walter Devereux, first earl of Essex, who died in Dublin in 1576. Essex became favourite with Elizabeth after the death of Leicester and disgrace of Raleigh. Praised by Spenser in dedicatory sonnet to *The*

Faerie Queene in 1596 and in *Prothelamion*. Believed to have been dedicatee of the *View* had it been published. Generally regarded as Spenser's last patron.

Devereux, Sir Walter, 1st earl of Essex and 2nd viscount Hereford (?1541–76), Irish adventurer. Active in suppression of northern rebellion in 1569. Made Knight of Garter and created earl of Essex in 1572. Undertook the colonisation of Ulster in 1573. He executed Sir Brian Mac Phelim in 1574, and was made earl-marshal in 1575. Recalled after Rathlin Island Massacre. Reappointed earl-marshal in 1576. After his death in Dublin the same year, he was rumoured to have been poisoned on the orders of the earl of Leicester, who subsequently married his widow.

Digges, Thomas (d. 1593), matriculated as a pensioner of Queen's College, Cambridge in May 1546. He duly proceeded BA five years later. Digges was a colleague of John Dee, whose mathematical genius he shared. Dee wrote the preface for Henry Billingsley's translation of Euclid's *Geometrie*. On the 14 April 1582 Digges was made a member of an advisory committee set up to review the fortifications at Dover. He married Agnes, a daughter of Sir Warham St Leger. It was probably during his courtship of Agnes that he came into contact with the select circle of colonial officials immortalised by Bryskett's *Discourse*.

Dillon, Sir Robert (d. 1597), was sworn in as Second Justice of the germinal presidency of Connaught on 15 June 1569. By virtue of the patronage of Lord Deputy Grey he was elevated to the office of Chief Justice on 28 June 1581, replacing his great-uncle Sir Robert Dillon (c.1500–80). One of Bryskett's Dublin guests.

Dormer, George, identified with 'M. Dormer the Queenes Sollicitor' in Bryskett's *Discourse*, an Oxford-educated lawyer, and a native of Ross in county Cork. It seems he wrote in ballad-royal *The Decaye of Rosse*, a tale, incidentally, narrated by Stanyhurst in Holinshed's *Chronicles*. He was made the Queen's Justice for Wexford on 17 July 1585.

Drayton, Michael (1563–31), the first major poet to be influenced by S. Drayton had no university education, but was widely read. He shared S's patriotism and commitment to pastoral. Drayton initially earned recognition as a disciple of S with *Idea: The Shepheards Garland* (1593), dedicated to Robert Dudley, sole son of the late Earl of Leicester. The nine eclogues resemble *SC* in form and content, replete with archaisms and Chaucerianisms. Drayton is thought to be the poet represented as 'Aetion' in *Col. The Tragicall Legend of Robert, Duke of Normandy* (entered in the Stationers' Register in November 1596, ten months after *FQ* IV–VI) opens with a personification of Isis, Thames and Medway, echoing the marriage of the rivers in *FQ* IV xi. *Poly-Olbion* (1612–22), a county-by-county poetic description of England and Wales, was issued in 1630, possibly without Drayton's consent, as *The Faerie Land*. Drayton often praised S. In his elegy to Henry Reynolds he styled him 'Grave morall *Spencer*'. Drayton was buried near Spenser in Westminster Abbey.

Drury, Sir William (1527–79), educated at Gonville Hall, Cambridge. Participated in siege of Boulogne in 1544. Served as marshal and deputy governor of Berwick from 1564 to 1576. Raided Scotland with Walter Devereux, 1st earl of Essex, in 1570. Knighted the same year. Appointed President of Munster in 1576, and Lord Justice of Ireland in 1578. Suppressed practice of coyne and livery.

Du Bartas, Seigneur Guillaume Saluste (1544–90), a Gascon Huguenot, author of influential radical Protestant treatises. Popular in France in the 1570s and 1580s, he sustained a reputation in Renaissance England due to the translations of Joshua Sylvester, earning the interest and admiration of individuals such as Philip Sidney and Gabriel Harvey. His *Sepmaines* may have inspired S's choice of the epic form for *FQ*.

Du Bellay, Joachim (1525–60), one of the most influential of the new French poets. His two most important works were the prose treatise *Defense et Illustration de la Langue Francaise* (1549), and his volume of Petrarchan sonnets, *Olive* (1552). In 1569, S contributed 'Visions of Du Bellay' to Jan Van Der Noot's *Theatre for Worldlings*.

Dudley, Robert, earl of Leicester (1532-1588), friend of Elizabeth before she was enthroned, he became a royal favourite. Knighted and made Master of the Horse upon her succession. Introduced to Spenser through the Sidneys and Harvey, he became, for a short time, an influential patron. Opposed French match for the Queen, his protestant sympathies compelling him to take a strong stance against the proposed marriage, straining relations with Elizabeth. Restored to favour in 1579, by which time Spenser had resolved to abandon court for colony. Having supported Henry Sidney and the Geraldine faction in Ireland, Leicester lost interest in that country with Sidney's retiral and the outbreak of the Desmond Rebellion (1579–83).

Dyer, Edward (1543–1607), poet, courtier and diplomat, now principally renowned as a companion of Philip Sidney and one of the 'Areopagus' referred to in the Spenser–Harvey correspondence. Spenser was 'in some use of familiarity' with Dyer during his stay in London between October 1579 and August 1580. Spenser told Harvey that he intended to dedicate his (lost) work *My Slomber* to Dyer.

Fenton, Sir Geoffrey (?1539–1608), translator and administrator, rendering a number of radical Protestant continental discourses into English during the 1570s. Best known for his last published work, a translation of Guicciardini's *History of the Wars of Italy* (1579). Fenton's older brother was a captain serving with Sir William Pelham's forces in Munster, and in 1580 Fenton followed his brother to Ireland. Pelham recommended him to Sir Francis Walsingham as a candidate for the Irish secretaryship, and on 22 July 1580, three weeks before Lord Grey's arrival in Dublin, Fenton wrote to Burghley from Limerick to say that he had secured that post. He remained as principal secretary in Ireland until his death in Dublin on 25 July 1608.

Fitzgerald, Gerald, 15th earl of Desmond (d. 1583), Old English lord who quarrelled constantly with Thomas Butler, 10th earl of Ormond. He was imprisoned from 1567 to 1573 for refusing to accept Sir Henry Sidney's favouring of Ormond. Rearrested on his return to Ireland, he escaped and entered into rebellion. He later submitted, rebelled again in 1579, was attainted and, with a price on his head, was killed in 1583. Spenser was among those who gained an estate from Desmond's demise.

Fitzgerald, Gerald, 11th earl of Kildare (1525–85), Old English noble educated in Verona, Mantua and Florence, serving with

Cosimo di Medici. Restored to his estates by Edward VII and to the earldom by Mary. Warred against the Irish and the Spanish invaders. He was imprisoned in the Tower on suspicion of Treason in 1582. On his release in 1584, he returned to Ireland. A patron of Richard Stanyhurst, and associate of the Leicester–Sidney Circle, he died in London in 1585.

Fitzwilliam, Sir William (1526–99), English official in Ireland, acting as vice-treasurer from 1559 to 1573. Served under the earl of Sussex against Shane O'Neill in 1561. Became Lord Justice in 1571, and Lord Deputy from 1572 to 1575. Reappointed in 1588. An active Privy Councillor in Ireland, he left the country in 1599.

Gerrard, Sir William (d. 1581), barrister at Gray's Inn in 1546, served as MP for Preston in 1553, and for Chester from 1555 to 1572. Named as Lord Chancellor of Ireland in April 1576. Knighted in 1577. An active member of the Irish Ecclesiastical Commission, he campaigned vigorously for judicial reform and wrote extensively on the state of Ireland.

Gilbert, Sir Humphrey (?1539–83), navigator, stepbrother of Sir Walter Raleigh, educated at Eton and Oxford, served under Sir Henry Sidney in Ireland. Given charge of Munster in 1569. Knighted in 1570, and made MP for Plymouth in 1571. Served under Perrot against Spanish naval force off Munster in 1579. Published in 1576 a *Discourse of a Discovery for a New Passage to Cataia*, edited by George Gascoigne. Turned his attention to New World voyages, and was lost in a storm off the southern Azores in 1583.

Googe, Barnaby (1540–94) was an Oxbridge product, studying at New College, Oxford and Christ's College, Cambridge. He appears, however, to have taken a degree at neither institution. He was patronised by his kinsman, William Cecil, later Lord Burghley. Author of *Eglogs, Epytaphs, and Sonettes* (1563), which, with those of Alexander Barclay, are the earliest example before *The Shepheardes Calender* of pastorals in English. Among his translations are *The Zodiake of Lyfe*, by Pierre Angelo Manzoni (1560); *The Popish Kingdome*, by Thomas Kirchmayer (1570), dedicated to Cecil; *Foure Bookes of Husbandrie*, by 'Conradus Heresbachius' (1577), dated from Kingston in Ireland, 1 February 1577, and dedicated to Sir

William Fitzwilliam. In 1574 Googe was sent to Ireland at Cecil's behest. In 1578 he had a prose-epistle prefixed to Barnaby Rich's *Allarme to England*. In 1582 he was made Provost Marshal of Connaught. Resigned and returned to England in 1585.

Greville, Fulke, Lord Brooke (1554–1628), poet, dramatist, radical protestant, humanist. Famous as a friend of Philip Sidney. Few biographers seem aware of the fact that Greville served in his youth under Lord Justice Pelham in Ireland. Joan Rees, in *The Spenser Encyclopedia* (pp. 340–1), speculates that 'Greville may have been abroad' in 1580 while S was associating with Sidney and Edward Dyer. A letter from Pelham to Walsingham dated from Limerick 14 July 1580 states 'Fulk Greville hurt in the leg.' It is quite feasible that Spenser knew both Greville and Sidney in Ireland. Greville is best known as the author of *A Treatie of Humane Learning* and *A Treatise of Religion*. His most notable literary work is the Senecan drama *Mustapha*. He was a puritan who saw redemption for 'Gods owne elect', and considered poetry and music to be 'Arts of Recreation'.

Grey, Arthur, Lord Grey de Wilton (1536–93), born in the English Pale in France. Employed under Cecil. Served in Scotland at the siege of Leith against the French. Became Lord Grey in 1562, residing at Whaddon House in Buckinghamshire. Appointed Lord Deputy of Ireland in 1580. Spenser served as his secretary, and received land and titles in return. Spenser was with Grey at Smerwick in November 1580 when the Spanish garrison was massacred. Grey's conduct was criticised. Grey was recalled from Ireland, on his own request, in 1582. Subsequently held minor appointments. Served as a commissioner at the trial of Mary Queen of Scots in 1587. Dedicatee of *The Faerie Queene*. Represented by Artegall in *FQ* V.

Grindal, Edmund, Archbishop of Canterbury (?1519–83), patron of John Young, whose consecration as Bishop of Rochester he presided over in 1578. Was himself appointed Archbishop of Canterbury on 10 January 1576. Within a year he had enraged Elizabeth by refusing to follow royal order forbidding 'prophesy-ings' – meetings to discuss Scripture. In a written response dated 20 December 1576, Grindal reminded the queen that she was 'a mortal creature' meddling in matters divine. In June 1577 Elizabeth suspended him for his disobedience. While he was out of favour, Spenser, in an implicit criticism of Elizabeth's treatment of Grindal, defended him in the anagrammatical figure of 'Algrind' in *Maye* 76 and *Julye* 128 of *SC*. Grindal was reconciled with the queen by the close of 1582, and died 6 July 1583.

Guarini, Giovanni Battista (1538–1612), court poet at Ferrara following the imprisonment of Tasso. Author of the immensely successful and widely read pastoral tragicomedy, *Il Pastor Fido* (1589), translated as *The Faithful Shepherd* in 1602, by which time it had gone through some twenty reprints. An Italian edition had been published in London as early as 1591. Believed by many to have influenced Spenser's narrative structure and style in *The Faerie Queene*.

Hanmer, Meredith (1543–1604), a native of England, educated at Christ Church, Oxford. He was installed as Archdeacon of Ross in 1591. From 1593 to 1604 he was Treasurer of Waterford; and from 1594 to 1604, Chanter's Vicar in Christ Church, Dublin. He was prebendary of St Michan's, Dublin from 1595 to 1602, warden of Youghal from 1598 to 1602, and from 1603 to 1604 he was Chancellor of St Canice, Kilkenny. Hanmer published a treatise against Edmund Campion in 1581, entitled *The Great Bragge and Challenge of Mr Champion, a Jesuit, answered*. Hanmer's contribution to Irish historiography, *A Chronicle of Ireland*, was published together with Spenser's *View* in Sir James Ware's *Two Histories of Ireland* in 1633.

Harington, John (1561–1612), courtier, adventurer and writer. His *Orlando Furioso in English Heroical Verse* (1591) is one of the most celebrated Elizabethan translations, an energetic and compelling version of Ariosto's original. Dedicated to his godmother, Queen Elizabeth, it won Harington a host of admirers, despite being derided by Ben Jonson. Harington shared with Spenser a liberal approach to Ariosto's text, and with both Spenser and Sidney a conviction that epic was the highest form of poetry in terms of its ability to teach morals. His Rabelaisian *The Metamorphosis of Ajax* (1596) has an 'Apologie' that refers to the complex rhyme scheme of *The Faerie Queene*, and an address to Sir John Spencer of Althorp which alludes to 'a learned Writer of your name'. Harington's commitment to epic poetry is often remarked, but a further parallel with Spenser is seldom noted. He was another courtly English writer with Irish interests. Based on his experiences, he composed 'A report of a journey into the North of Ireland written to Justice Carey' (1599) and 'A short view of the state of Ireland in 1605'.

Harvey, Gabriel (1550–1631), fellow of Pembroke Hall, and later of Trinity Hall, Cambridge. Early friend and mentor of Spenser, appearing as 'Hobbinol' in the pastorals. Published *Letters* and works in Latin. A keen scholar who disputed with university wits. Entered into heated public debate with Thomas Nashe, both authors eventually being censured. Copious annotator of texts. Often regarded as ambitious and self-absorbed, but this image owes much to Nashe's polemical attacks. Author of commendatory sonnet for *The Faerie Queene*, as well as recipient of dedicatory sonnet.

Hatton, Sir Christopher (1540–91), English courtier, patron of Barnaby Rich, among others. Educated at Oxford and the Inner Temple. By 1564 had won Elizabeth's admiration because of his dancing. Appointed Lord Chancellor in 1587. One of the original Munster undertakers along with Spenser. Dedicatee of *The Faerie Queene*.

Herbert, Sir William (?1553–93), English planter, author, and scholar. On 14 February 1588, he wrote to Walsingham that he wished to leave to posterity 'a volume of my writing', 'a colony of my planting' and 'a college of my erecting'. He managed only the first two. Herbert, like Spenser, became an 'undertaker' in the Munster plantation on 5 May 1586, and applied the next month for three 'seignories' in Co. Kerry. Herbert was granted property amounting to 13,276 acres. Around 1588 he acted as vice-president of Munster in the absence of Sir Thomas Norris. He returned to England in the spring of 1589, and died there in March 1593. Herbert was the author of a Latin treatise on Ireland entitled *Croftus; sive de Hibernia Liber*, named after Sir James Croft, who had served as Lord Deputy of Ireland from 1551 to 1552.

Howard, Charles, Lord Howard of Effingham, and earl of Nottingham (1536–1624), English sailor and cousin of the Queen, who in 1573 succeeded his father. Made lord high admiral in 1585, and in 1588 commanded the English navy against the Armada.

Created an earl after Cadiz. Dedicatee of *The Faerie Queene*. Suppressed Essex Rebellion in 1601.

Kirke, Edward (1553–1613), identified with 'E. K.', author of the epistle to Harvey and the textual apparatus of *SC*. E. K. is often conjectured to be S himself, but other critics believe the initials to signify Edward Kirke, who became a sizar at Pembroke Hall in 1571, making him a close contemporary of S. Kirke received his BA in 1575 and MA in 1578 (two years after S), and then became rector at Risby, Suffolk in 1580. S's reference of 16 October 1579, in *Two Letters*, to having been that morning at 'Mystresse *Kerkes*' lends substance to the identification.

Kyd, Thomas (?1557–?95), dramatist, educated at Merchant Taylors' School. Originally a scrivener. His *Spanish Tragedy* was printed in 1594. *Cornelia* was licensed the same year. Possibly the author of a pre-Shakespearean *Hamlet*, not extant. His *First Part of Ieronimo* was published in 1605. Kyd was one of the best-known tragic poets of his time.

Lodge, Thomas (1558–1625), poet, dramatist and translator. Pupil at Merchant Taylors' School (1571–3) while Mulcaster was Headmaster, but after Spenser's time there. Literary career from 1579 to 1597 coincides with Spenser's. He left England a Catholic recusant in 1597 and subsequently studied medicine in Avignon. Author of *Rosalynde* (1590), his best-known work, inspired by *The Shepheardes Calender*, and a sonnet sequence entitled *Phillis* (1593). Refers to Spenser by name in *Wits Miserie and the Worlds Madnesse* (1596). May feature as 'Alcon' in *Colin Clouts Come Home Againe* 394–5. By no means a Spenserian, but clearly influenced by Spenser.

Loftus, Adam (1533–1605), second son of Edward Loftus of Yorkshire, matriculated at Trinity College, Cambridge in 1556. Became chaplain to Lord Lieutenant Sussex in 1560. Nominated to archbishopric of Armagh in 1561. Made Dean of St Patrick's in Dublin in 1565. From 1567 to his death, served as archbishop of Dublin. Served as Lord Justice of Ireland in 1582, 1597 and 1599. Led establishment of Trinity College, Dublin, and served as its first provost.

Long, John (1548–89), another of the guests at Bryskett's house, born in London and educated first at Eton then at King's College, Cambridge, where he was admitted as a scholar on 13 August 1564. He became Primate of all Ireland on 13 July 1584 having been nominated by Perrot one week earlier. He was admitted to the Privy Council in Ireland within a year of securing the Primacy. Long died at Drogheda in 1589.

Lyon, William (d. 1617), Bishop of Cork, who married Edmund Spenser to Elizabeth Boyle, a kinswoman of the great earl of Cork, in 1594. Lyon had been in Ireland in the late 1570s, and had served under Lord Grey as army chaplain in the early 1580s.

Malby, Sir Nicholas (?1530–84), native of Yorkshire, went to Ireland with Sidney in 1565 and served as sergeant major of the army. Posted to Carrickfergus in Ulster with Captain William Piers to check progress of Scots from 1567 to 1569. Collector of customs at Strangford, Ardglass, and Dundrum in 1571, he made unsuccessful efforts to settle part of Down from 1571 to 1574. Became Privy Councillor in Ireland in 1575. Knighted and appointed Colonel of Connaught province in 1576, he published 'a cure for a foundered horse' the same year. Made President of Connaught in 1579, and acted as military commander in Munster during sickness of Sir William Drury that year. Engaged in suppressing Desmond Rebellion from 1579-81. A vociferous proponent of forceful reform and plantation in Ireland.

Mulcaster, Richard (?1530–1611), born at Brackenhall Castle on the Scottish border, educated at Eton and Christ Church, Oxford, he became a London schoolmaster. First Headmaster of Merchant Taylors' School (1561–86). Accomplished linguist and eloquent proponent of the English language. It is not clear how much direct contact he had with Spenser at school, or how far Spenser followed Mulcaster's theories of language. As a radical humanist and a champion of the vernacular he must have exerted some influence over the poet.

Munster Undertakers (1587–95). There were thirty-five successful undertakers, or planters, including Spenser, who received letters patent in this period in the Munster plantation. Some of these have been dealt with elsewhere, but the full list, excluding Spenser, is given here: Robert Cullum, George Thornton, William Carter, Sir

George Bourchier, Sir Warham St Leger, Jenkin Conway, Francis Barkley, Robert Annesley, Sir Walter Raleigh, Edward Denny, Thomas Butler (the earl of Ormond), Sir Christopher Hatton, George Stone, Sir Valentine Brown, Sir Edward Fitton, Arthur Robbins, Thomas Norris, Richard Beacon, Thomas Saye, Henry Oughtred, Henry Billingsley, Phane Becher, Hugh Cuffe, Sir William Courtenay, Robert Strode, William Trenchard, Edmund Mainwaring, Hugh Worth, Thomas Fleetwood, Marmaduke Redmayne, Arthur Hyde, Sir William Herbert, Charles Herbert and Denzil Holles.

Noot, Jan van der (*c*.1538–1601), born in Brecht near Antwerp, became a Calvinist in 1566 and fled to England the following year. Arrived in London in April 1567, leading a group of Antwerp protestants, with a letter of safe passage from William of Orange to William Cecil. Published French, Dutch and English editions of his *Theatre for Worldlings*, to which Spenser contributed his 'Epigrams' and 'Sonets'. His publisher, Henry Bynneman, also produced Sir Thomas Smith's Irish pamphlet of 1572, the Spenser–Harvey correspondence, and work by Geoffrey Fenton and Richard Stanyhurst. Van der Noot was the first major Dutch Renaissance poet, and his innovative style, metrical experiments, and pre-occupation with emblems and woodcuts evidently inspired Spenser.

Norris, John (*c*.1547–97), one of the sons of Sir Henry Norris. Served as Lord President of Munster. Fought with the Huguenots in France, and with the earl of Leicester in the Low Countries. Served as MP for Cork in 1586 Dublin parliament. Commanded Portugese expedition, along with Sir Frances Drake, in 1589.

Norris, Sir Thomas (1556-1599), entered Magdalene College, Oxford in 1571, and graduated BA on 6 April 1576. By December 1579 he was considered sufficiently mature, at the tender age of twenty-three, to lead a troop of horse in Ireland at the outbreak of the Desmond Rebellion. In August 1582, Norris was made colonel of the forces in Munster. Two years later, he was embroiled in Perrot's campaign against the MacDonnells of Antrim. From 1585 to 1586 he was the MP for Limerick, and in December 1586 he was appointed acting President of Munster in lieu of his brother, John, whilst the latter was engaged with the earl of Leicester and Sir

Philip Sidney in the Netherlands. Another of Bryskett's Dublin guests.

O'Neill, Hugh (The O'Neill), earl of Tyrone (1550–1616), an orphan of the O'Neills, subject of a family feud, brought up in England as a friend of Sir Henry Sidney. Returned to Ireland and was adopted as scourge of the English planters, ironic given his courtly background. Leader of the Tyrone Rebellion, the uprising that led to the overthrow of the Munster plantation and the destruction of Spenser's estate.

Pelham, Sir William (d. 1587), Lord Justice of Ireland, sent there in the summer of 1579 to fortify the Pale against the threat of incursions by the O'Neills. Knighted by Sir William Drury, whom he succeeded, on the latter's death, as Lord Justice. Pelham provoked Elizabeth's displeasure by proclaiming the earl of Desmond a traitor and leaving the prosecution of the war against him to his rival, the earl of Ormond. In January 1580 he set out for Munster himself to ward off a rumoured Spanish landing at Dingle. Conducted a merciless campaign against the Irish rebels, massacring the garrison at Carrigafoyle Castle on 27 March. Establishing his headquarters at Limerick, he proceeded to garrison the province and to starve the rebels into submission. At news of Grey's arrival in Dublin, Pelham prepared to greet the incoming Lord Deputy. He was apparently offended by Spenser's lack of courtesy. He surrendered the sword of state to Grey on 7 September in St Patrick's Cathedral. Mooted as a possible president of Munster, he finally left Ireland in October 1580, after an eventful year. Identified with Sergis in *The Faerie Queene*.

Percy, Henry, 9th earl of Northumberland (1564–1632), dedicatee of *The Faerie Queene*. A friend of Sir Walter Raleigh, he was known as the 'Wizard Earl' for his interest in the new sciences, such as alchemy.

Perrot, Sir John (1527–92), reputedly a bastard son of Henry VIII, assumed name of Thomas Perrot of Pembrokeshire. Knighted in 1547. Imprisoned for Protestant views under Mary. Appointed President of Council in Munster in 1570. Favoured military policy in Ireland. In 1579, led squadron of ships to Ireland to police waters of south-west, amid reports of Spanish invasion. (Lord

Grey subsequently defeated the Spanish at Smerwick.) Perrot returned to Ireland in 1584 as Lord Deputy to oversee Munster settlement. Recalled in 1588 and incarcerated in Tower of London. Found guilty of slandering Elizabeth. Died prior to sentencing.

Ponsonby, William (*c.*1547–1604), a London Stationer regarded as one of the most influential of the Elizabethan publishers. Best known as publisher and seller of Spenser and Sidney during the 1590s. Both the 1590 and 1596 editions of *The Faerie Queene* bear his imprint, as do *Complaints, Daphnaida, Amoretti and Epithalamion, Colin Clouts Come Home Againe, Fowre Hymnes,* and *Prothalamion.* Ponsonby intervened actively in the works he produced, collaborating with Spenser on the first edition of *The Faerie Queene,* writing his own preface for *Complaints,* in which he made a commitment to publish Spenser's lost works, and dedicating *Amoretti,* while Spenser was in Ireland, to Sir Robert Needham. Built a reputation for radical protestant literature associated with the Leicester–Sidney Circle. Started trading officially in 1577, and brought off a double coup in 1590 with publication of authorised version of Sidney's *Old Arcadia* and first three books of *The Faerie Queene.* Followed this with 1593 *Arcadia* and the authorized *Defence of Poetry* in 1595. Books three to six of *The Faerie Queene* appeared in 1596, and two years later Ponsonby published the first collected edition of Sidney's works. The same year, he was appointed Warden of the Stationers' Company.

Raleigh, Sir Walter (1552–1618), born in the west country and educated at Oxford, he served with Lord Grey in Ireland, with whom he had a fraught relationship. It was in Ireland, at Smerwick and throughout the Munster campaign, that Raleigh made Spenser's acquaintance. Returning to England in 1581, he became Elizabeth's first favourite for the next ten years. Knighted in 1583, he was made Captain of the Queen's Guard in 1587. Undertaker in Munster plantation, strengthening his ties with Spenser, who penned his 'Letter to Raleigh' to accompany the first three books of *The Faerie Queene.* Raleigh was the author of two commendatory sonnets and the addressee of a dedicatory sonnet. Subsequently disgraced at court, he was superseded by Essex as favourite until 1596. Thereafter, he lost interest in Ireland and turned his attention to the New World.

Rich, Barnaby (1542–1617), author and soldier, served in army from war with France in 1557–8. Sailed to Ireland with Walter Devereaux, first earl of Essex, on 17 July 1573. Took part in attempts to colonise Ulster. Thereafter spent much of his time around Dublin. From 1574 began to publish a series of popular treatises. In 1584, with Perrot installed as Lord Deputy, Rich had one hundred men under his command at Coleraine. Wrote numerous descriptions of Ireland. Rich was, in his own words, brought up 'in the fields among unlettered soldiers'.

Rogers, Daniel (?1538–91), diplomat, born in Wittenberg. He came to England in 1548 and was naturalised in 1552. Studied at Wittenberg and Oxford, taking his BA in 1561. Secretary of the Fellowship of English Merchants at Antwerp in 1575. Engaged in diplomatic business in the Low Countries from 1567 to 1568. In 1579, Rogers became one of the so-called Areopagus (court of ancient Athens), a putative literary coterie surrounding Philip Sidney, whose members included Spenser, Harvey, Thomas Drant, and Edward Dyer. Mission to Duke of Saxony in 1580. Arrested on imperial territory and imprisoned until *c.*1584. Made clerk of the Privy Council in 1587.

Ronsard, Pierre De (1524–85), aristocratic poet and humanist, prominent in high Renaissance French poetry. Placed great faith in French language as a poetic medium. Mainly known for his lyric and elegaic work. His attempt at epic, in the *Franciade*, earned him few accolades. Spenser emulated his sombre commitment to poetry and his expert handling of metre.

Sackville, Thomas, Lord Buckhurst, 1st earl of Dorset (1536–1608), English poet and statesman, entered parliament in 1558, the year Elizabeth succeeded the throne. A cousin of the Queen, he contributed *The Induction* and *Buckingham* to *The Myrroure for Magistrates* (1563). Knighted in 1567, and created Lord Buckhurst. Served as a diplomat in France and the Low Countries. Announced death sentence to Mary Queen of Scots. Made a Knight of the Garter in 1589. Recipient of one of Spenser's dedicatory sonnets accompanying *The Faerie Queene*. Became Lord High Treasurer in 1599, and earl of Dorset in 1604.

Sidney, Sir Henry (1529–86), eldest son and heir of Sir William

Sidney, chamberlain and steward of prince Edward's household. Raised with the prince. Knighted in 1550. Married Mary, daughter of John Dudley, duke of Northumberland, in 1551. Sidney was appointed to his first post in Ireland in 1556, serving as vice-treasurer. Member of Privy Council there. Succeeded Sussex as Lord Deputy in 1565. Over next two years, Sidney presided over defeat of Shane O'Neill and establishment of provincial councils and Court of Star Chamber in Dublin. Reappointed Lord Deputy in 1568, and again in 1575. Left Ireland for last time in 1578, discredited due to military overspending. Son Philip mentioned as possible successor. In 1582, there was talk of reappointing Sidney, and he included among his conditions for assuming the post again the proviso that his son Philip should accompany him and succeed him in the office.

Sidney, Mary, Countess of Pembroke, sister of Philip, married Henry Herbert, 2nd earl of Pembroke in 1577. Important patroness and translator. Dedicatee of *The Faerie Queene*. Figures as Urania in *Colin Clouts Come Home Againe* and as Clorinda in 'Astrophel'.

Sidney, Sir Philip (1554–86), eldest son of Sir Henry Sidney, soldier, statesman and poet. Educated at Oxford and on the continent. On 19 August 1570, Elizabeth wrote to Philip's father, Sir Henry Sidney, the Irish viceroy, declining his request that Philip join him in Ireland, on the grounds that the plague was prevalent there. Philip did travel to Ireland in 1576, and was in Dublin shortly after the death of the first earl of Essex in 1576. In September 1577 he composed a paper designed to vindicate his father's conduct in Ireland. In July 1578 he met Gabriel Harvey at Audley End. Harvey introduced him to S. At the end of 1578 S was Leicester's guest in London at Leicester House, and Sidney probably met him there. Dedicatee of *Shepheardes Calender* (1579). Elected MP for Kent in 1581. Appointed 'general of the horse' in 1585. Married Frances, daughter of Sir Francis Walsingham, on 20 September 1583. Knighted the same year. On 21 September 1585 Elizabeth appointed him Governor of Flushing. At the same time Leicester was made commander-in-chief in the Low Countries. Sidney died after being wounded in action, on 17 October 1586. Eight elegies on Sidney, including S's own 'Astrophel: A Pastorall Elegie', appended to *Colin Clouts Come Home Againe* in 1595.

Singleton, Hugh (d. 1593), the printer of the first edition of *The Shepheardes Calender*. May have learned his craft in a continental printing house. Published his first book in 1544. Acquired reputation as publisher of radical protestant literature. Became infamous in 1579 by publishing John Stubbs's *Discoverie of a Gaping Gulf* attacking the projected royal match between Elizabeth and the Duc 'd'Alençon. The book outraged Elizabeth, Stubbs lost his right hand, and Singleton was fortunate not to lose his. Unlike Ponsonby, Singleton did not sustain a professional relationship with Spenser. *The Shepheardes Calender* was assigned to John Harrison the younger on 29 October 1580, and published by Thomas East in 1581. Despite his involvement in the Stubbs affair, Singleton's career progressed when he replaced John Day as official printer to the City of London on 4 April 1584. His last book was entered in the Stationers' Register on 31 March 1592.

Smith, Thomas, apothecary, another guest of Bryskett's. What scant information there is concerning 'M. Smith the Apothecary' describes him as the compiler, around 1561, of a dossier on the Gaelic bards, familiar subjects of scorn for the literati of the Dublin administration. The aim of Smith's catalogue of crimes endorsed or encouraged by the bards was to justify legislation targeted against the praise poets.

Smith, Sir Thomas (1513–77), diplomat, linguist and political theorist, is mentioned by name in E. K.'s gloss on the January Eclogue for the word 'couthe': 'couthe) commeth of the verbe Conne, that is, to know or to have skill. As well interpreteth the same the worthy Sir Tho. Smith in his booke of goverment: wherof I have a perfect copie in wryting, lent me by his kinsman, and my verye singular good freend, M. Gabriel Harvey: as also of some other his most grave and excellent wrytings.' The 'booke of goverment' to which E. K. refers is Smith's *De Republica Anglorum*, written before 1565, but not published until 1581. The 'other his most grave and excellent wrytings' indubitably includes the promotional pamphlet commissioned by Smith in support of the colonial venture he undertook early in the 1570s with his son of the same name. Smith's pamphlet was published in 1572 by Henry Bynneman, the same publisher who had produced Geoffrey Fenton's *Discourse of the civile warres in Fraunce* (1570) and *Actes of conference in religion* (1571), and who later published Harvey and

Spenser's *Three proper, wittie and familiar letters* (1580), and, in 1583, the English edition of Richard Stanyhurst's *Translation of he first four books of the Aeneis*. In June 1565, Smith had written to Cecil on the question of Ireland, complaining that: 'For this two hundred years not one hath taken the right way to make that country either subject or profitable'. The so-called 'Ulster Project' promised a solution to the problem. Smith, whose elegant marketing of the whole operation is amply evident in the promotional pamphlet of 1572, gave it the stamp of official approval.

Stanyhurst, Richard (1547–1618), a Dubliner by birth, was educated at Kilkenny in Ireland and at Oxford, where he arrived in 1563. He was admitted BA five years later. As an Oxford undergraduate he made the acquaintance of Edmund Campion. Afterwards, he studied law in London, initially at Furnivall's Inn, then at Lincoln's Inn. He returned to Dublin in the company of Campion. It was during this stay in Dublin that the Stanyhursts, Campion and Sidney were acquainted. When Holinshed commissioned him for the Irish section of the *Chronicles*, Stanyhurst submitted a revised version of Campion's *History*, which he dedicated to Lord Deputy Sidney. Among his sources, he cites Bale and Giraldus Cambrensis. Stanyhurst's *Translation of The first Four books of P. Virgilius Maro* (1582) had much calumny heaped upon it, but it was praised in 1592 by Harvey, who was returning the compliment paid him by Stanyhurst in the preface to the *Four books*. Writing in June 1582, Stanyhurst makes a direct reference to Harvey's metrical theories in 'one of his familiar letters'. The Spenser–Harvey correspondence was published by Bynneman, Stanyhurst's English publisher. In 1598, Francis Meres could 'name but two Iambical Poets, Gabriel Harvey and Richard Stanyhurst'. Stanyhurst was both criticised and plagiarised in the *View*.

St Leger, Sir Warham (1525–97), another of Bryskett's guests, second son of Lord Deputy Sir Anthony St Leger. Obtained favour of Sir Henry Sidney and was made member of Privy Council in Ireland in 1565, knighted in the same year, and nominated as first president of council in Munster. Rejected as President of Munster a year after his nomination. Resided at Cork. Sided with Desmond against Ormond, to dissatisfaction of the queen. Left for England in 1569. Returned to Ireland in 1579 as Provost Marshal of Munster.

Served briefly as commander-in-chief in Munster during Desmond Rebellion in 1581. Beneficiary of Munster Plantation. Died at Cork in 1597, having been in Munster for the bulk of his political career.

Tasso, Torquato (1544–95), Italian poet whose *Jerusalem Delivered from the Turk* fulfilled his early promise and established his reputation as a leading Renaissance author. Illness ended his literary career in 1579, the very year that Spenser launched his own with *The Shepheardes Calender*.

Travers, John (d. 1618), husband of Sarah, Spenser's sister. Registrar of the Diocese of Cork, Cloyne and Ross. Appointed Commissary of the Victuals, with Carrickfergus as his head-quarters, in March 1599.

Ubaldini, Petruccio (?1524–?1600), illuminator and scholar, born Tuscany, came to England in 1545, and entered the service of the crown. Saw action in Scottish war under Sir James Croft, Governor of Haddington in 1549. In 1551 he wrote a text on English culture and society, mapping out the manners, customs and institutions of his adopted country. In 1580 he was present at Smerwick when the garrison was massacred, and composed an account which suggests that a secretary of Lord Grey, possibly Spenser, profited financially from the event by accepting a bribe or ransom. In 1581 Ubaldini authored the first Italian book printed in England.

Vere, Edward de, 17th earl of Oxford, Elizabethan court poet, Italianate Englishman, hereditary Lord Great Chamberlain of England, literary patron, and dedicatee of *The Faerie Queene*.

Walsingham, Sir Francis (*c*.1532–90), English statesman, born in Kent, educated at King's College, Cambridge. Sent on embassy to France by Burghley (1570–3). His expertise saw him appointed one of Elizabeth's principal secretaries of state. Completed missions in the Netherlands (1578), France (1581) and Scotland (1583). Ran a highly efficient spy network. One of commissioners who tried Mary Queen of Scots at Fotheringhay. Sympathetic to Puritan party. Dedicatee of *The Faerie Queene*. His daughter Frances married in turn Philip Sidney, the earl of Essex and Richard de Burgh, fourth earl of Clanricarde.

Watts, Thomas, Archdeacon of Middlesex (*c.*1528–*c.*1577), associate of Grindal and Young and alleged patron of Spenser (see Judson, 1939). Matriculated as a pensioner at Christ's College, Cambridge, in November 1549. Took his BA 1552–3. Exiled with other English Protestants in Frankfurt in 1557. Back in England in 1559. On 1 January 1560 attains first preferment, as prebend of Tottenham – later Tottenham Court – in St Paul's. Made deacon on 23 March, and priest on 24 March, by Grindal, now bishop of London. Takes his MA this same year. On 31 January 1561 Watts was collated Archdeacon of Middlesex following resignation of Nowell. On 13 August he was appointed Twelfth Stall of Westminster, and installed on 3 November. Between 1562 and 1565 he took part in at least two visitations to Merchant Taylors'. On 20 August 1570 he was made rector of Bocking, Essex, by Archbishop Parker. Raised to dean of same on 5 April 1571. From 4 November 1572 Watts shares this office with John Still, rector of Hadleigh, Suffolk. Judson believes Watts to have been behind Spenser's admission to Cambridge.

Young, John, Bishop of Rochester (1534–1605), served as Master of Pembroke Hall (1567–78) during Spenser's time at Cambridge, including a spell as vice-chancellor in 1569. Earlier in his career he had been chaplain to Archbishop Grindal, and in 1578 Grindal oversaw his consecration as Bishop of Rochester in Kent. A note in Harvey's copy of Jerome Turler's *Traveiler* (1575) shows that Spenser served as Young's secretary. Young figures in the September Eclogue of *The Shepheardes Calender* as 'Roffynn' or 'Roffy'. Hobbinol (Harvey) compliments Roffynn and names Colin, Spenser's poetic persona, as 'his self boye'. Spenser was back in London according to Harvey by 10 July 1579, suggesting that Spenser's secretaryship under Young, and, as far as is known, his association with him, had ended by this date. Spenser may well have composed most of *The Shepheardes Calender* in Kent, accounting in part for its preoccupation with pastoral affairs.

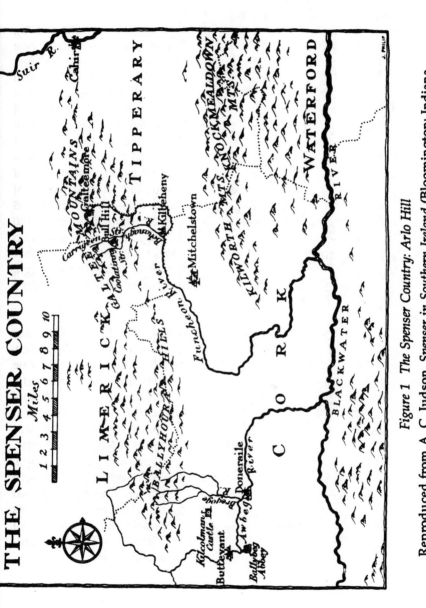

Figure 1 The Spenser Country: Arlo Hill

Reproduced from A. C. Judson, *Spenser in Southern Ireland* (Bloomington: Indiana University Press, 1933) p. 59

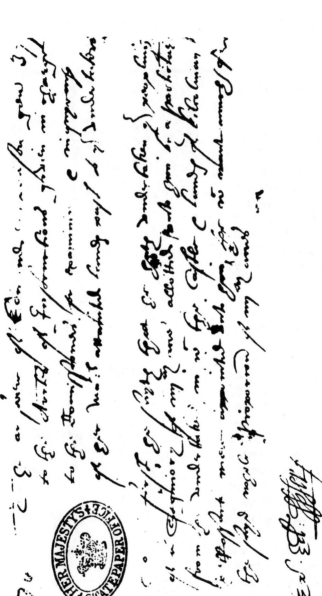

Figure 2 Spenser's signature

Reproduced from the opening of Spenser's answer to *Articles*, May 1589, *State Papers, Ireland* (PRO, London)

Select Bibliography

1. Bibliographical Material

Atkinson, D. F., *Edmund Spenser: A Bibliographical Supplement* (Baltimore: Johns Hopkins University Press, 1937).

McNier, W. F. and F. Provost, *Edmund Spenser: An Annotated Bibliography*, 2nd edn (Sussex: Harvester Press, 1975).

Maley, Willy, 'Spenser and Ireland: A Select Bibliography', *Spenser Studies*, 9 (1991) 227–42.

Vondersmith, B. J., 'A Bibliography of Criticism of *The Faerie Queene*, 1900–1970', in R. C. Frushell and B. J. Vondersmith (eds), *Contemporary Thought on Edmund Spenser* (Carbondale and Edwardsville, 1975) pp. 150–213.

2. Biographical Sources

Craik, G. L., *Spenser and his Poetry* (London, 1845).

Church, R. W., *Spenser* (London: Macmillan, 1879).

Collier, J. P., 'The Life of Spenser', in *The Works of Edmund Spenser*, vol. 1 (London: Bell and Daldy, 1862) pp. xvii–clxxviii.

de Selincourt, E., 'Introduction: Biographical and Critical', in J. C. Smith and E. de Selincourt (eds), *Spenser: Poetical Works* (Oxford: Oxford University Press, 1912) pp. vii–xl.

Grosart, A. B., *The Townley MSS: The Spending of the Money of Robert Nowell of Reade Hall, Lancashire: Brother of Dean Alexander Nowell. 1568–1580* (Manchester: privately printed, 1877).

——, *The Life of Edmund Spenser*, in *The Works of Edmund Spenser*, vol. 1 (1882).

Judson, A. C., 'Thomas Watts, Archdeacon of Middlesex (and Edmund Spenser)', *Indiana University Publications Humanities Series*, no. 2 (Bloomington, Ind.: Indiana University Press, 1939).

——, *The Life of Edmund Spenser*, in Greenlaw *et al.* (eds), *The Works of Edmund Spenser: A Variorum Edition*, 11 vols (Baltimore: Johns Hopkins University Press, 1932–49) vol. 11 (1945).

Watson, E. P. (ed.), Introduction to *Spenser: Selected Writings* (London: Routledge, 1992).

3. Reference Works

Attwater, A., *Pembroke College, Cambridge* (Cambridge: Cambridge University Press, 1936).

Calendar of Fiants Elizabeth (Dublin, 1875–90).

Calender of State Papers Relating to Ireland, 1509–73, 24 vols (London, 1867–1912).

Carpenter, F. I., *A Reference Guide to Edmund Spenser* (Chicago: Chicago University Press, 1923).

Ellis, Steven G., 'Framework of Events', in *Tudor Ireland: Crown, Community and the Conflict of Cultures, 1470–1603* (London and New York: Longman) pp. 1–11.

Greenlaw *et al.*, *The Works of Edmund Spenser: A Variorum Edition* (Baltimore: Johns Hopkins University Press, 1932–49).

Hamilton, A. C. (ed.), *Spenser: The Faerie Queene* (London and New York: Longman, 1977).

—— (ed.), *The Spenser Encyclopedia* (London: Routledge, 1990).

Jones, H. S. V., *A Spenser Handbook* (New York: Cornell University Press, 1930) pp. 377–87.

Moody, T. W., F. X. Martin and F. J. Byrne (eds), 'Chronology', in *A New History of Ireland, Early Modern Ireland* (Oxford: Clarendon Press, 1982) pp. 195–253.

Report of Historical Manuscripts Commission, 9th Report Appendix (1888) Cecil Papers, Hatfield MSS Part II.

Shepherd, Simon, 'Chronology', in *Spenser* (Sussex: Harvester Press, 1989) pp. 120–3.

Wells, William (ed.), *Spenser Allusions in the Sixteenth and Seventeenth Centuries*, compiled by R. Heffner, D. E. Mason and F. M. Padelford (Chapel Hill: The University of North Carolina Press, 1972).

4. Spenser and Ireland

Buck, P. M., 'New Facts Concerning the Life of Edmund Spenser', *Modern Language Notes*, vol. 19 (1904) 237–8.

Carpenter, F. I. 'Desiderata in the Study of Spenser', *Studies in Philology*, vol. 19 (1922) 238–43.

——, 'Spenser in Ireland', *Modern Philology*, vol. 19 (1922) 405–19.

Coleman, J., 'The Poet Spenser's Wife', *Journal of the Cork Historical and Archaeological Society*, 2nd ser., vol. 1 (1895) 131–3.

Covington, F. F., 'Spenser in Ireland', Yale University, unpublished Ph.D. thesis (1924).

Crino, A. M., 'La Relazione Barducci–Ubaldini Sull'Impresa D'Irlanda (1579–1581)', *English Miscellany*, vol. 19 (1968) 339–67.

Crowley, S., 'Some of Spenser's Doneraile Neighbours', *North Cork Writers Journal*, vol. 1 (1985) 71–5.

Draper, J. W., 'Edmund Spenser', *Journal of the Cork Historical and Archaeological Society*, vol. 3 (1894) 89–100.

Falkiner, C. L., 'Spenser in Ireland', in *Essays Relating to Ireland: Biographical, Historical, and Topographical* (London, 1909) pp. 3–31.

Ferguson, James F., 'Memorials of Edmund Spenser, the Poet, and his Descendants in the County Cork, from the Public Records of Ireland', *Journal of the Cork Historical and Archaeological Society*, vol. 14 (1908) 39–43.

Gottfried, R. B., 'Spenser and Stanyhurst', *The Times Literary Supplement*, vol. 35 (31 October 1936) 887.

——, 'The Date of Spenser's *View*', *Modern Language Notes*, vol. 52 (1937) 176-180.

——, 'Spenser's *View* and Essex', *PMLA*, vol. 52 (1937) 645–51.

—— (ed.), *The Works of Edmund Spenser: A Variorum Edition*, 11 vols, (Baltimore: Johns Hopkins University Press, 1932-1949) vol. 9: *The Prose Works* (1949).

Gray, M. M., 'The Influence of Spenser's Irish Experiences on The Faerie Queene', *Review of English Studies*, vol. 6 (1930) 413–28.

——, 'Review of Pauline Henley, *Spenser in Ireland*', *Modern Language Notes*, vol. 45 (1930) 320–3.

Heffner, Ray, 'Spenser's Acquisition of Kilcolman', *Modern Language Notes*, vol. 46 (1931) 493–8.

——, 'Essex and Book Five of *The Faerie Queene*', *English Literary History*, vol. 3 (1936) 67–82.

Henley, Pauline, *Spenser in Ireland* (Cork: Cork University Press, 1928).

Hennessey, J. P., 'Sir Walter Raleigh in Ireland', *Nineteenth Century*, vol. 10 (1881) 660–82.

——, *Sir Walter Raleigh in Ireland* (London, 1883).

Hore, H. F. (ed.), 'Sir Henry Sidney's Memoir of his Government of Ireland, 1583', *Ulster Journal of Archaeology*, vol. 3 (1856) 33–52, 85–109, 336–57; vol. 5 (1857) 299–323; vol. 8 (1860) 179–95.

Hulbert, V. B., 'Spenser's Relation to Certain Documents on Ireland', *Modern Philology*, vol. 34 (1937) 345–53.

Jardine, Lisa, 'Mastering the Uncouth: Gabriel Harvey, Edmund

Spenser and the English Experience in Ireland', in J. Henry and S. Hutton (eds), *New Perspectives on Renaissance Thought: Essays in Honour of Charles Schmitt* (London: Duckworth, 1990) pp. 68–82.

Jenkins, Raymond, 'Spenser and the Clerkship in Munster', *PMLA*, vol. 47 (1932) 109–21.

——, 'Spenser's Hand', *The Times Literary Supplement*, vol. 31 (7 January 1932) 12.

——, 'Spenser at Smerwick', *The Times Literary Supplement*, vol. 32 (11 May 1933) 331.

——, '*Newes out of Munster*, a Document in Spenser's Hand', *Studies in Philology*, vol. 32 (1935) 125–30.

——, 'Spenser with Lord Grey in Ireland', *PMLA*, vol. 52 (1937) 338–53.

——, 'Spenser: The Uncertain Years 1584–1589', *PMLA*, vol. 53 (1938) 350–62.

——, 'Spenser and Ireland', in W. R. Meuller and D. C. Allen (eds), *That Soveraine Light: Essays in Honor of Edmund Spenser 1552–1952* (Baltimore: Johns Hopkins University Press, 1952) pp. 51–62.

Jones, W., 'Doneraile and Vicinity', *Journal of the Cork Historical and Archaeological Society*, vol. 7 (1901) 238–42.

Judson, Alexander C., *Spenser in Southern Ireland* (Bloomington: Indiana University Press, 1933).

——, 'Two Spenser Leases', *Modern Language Quarterly*, vol. 50 (1944) 143–7.

——, 'Spenser and the Munster Officials', *Studies in Philology*, vol. 44 (1947) 157–73.

Koller, K., 'Spenser and Raleigh', *English Literary History*, vol. 1 (1934) 37–60.

Lewis, C. S., 'Spenser's Irish Experiences and *The Faerie Queene*', *Review of English Studies*, vol. 7 (1931) 83–5.

Lysaght, S., 'Kilcolman Castle', *The Antiquary*, vol. 5 (1882) 153–6.

McLane, Paul E., 'Was Spenser in Ireland in Early November 1579?', *Notes and Queries*, vol. 204 (1959) 99–101.

Mac Lir, M., 'Spenser as High Sheriff of Cork County', *Journal of the Cork Historical and Archaeological Society*, vol. 7 (1901) 249–50.

Maley, Willy, 'Review of A. C. Hamilton (gen. ed.), *The Spenser Encyclopedia*', *Textual Practice*, vol. 6(3) (1992) 543–9.

Martin, W. C., 'The Date and Purpose of Spenser's *Veue*', *PMLA*, vol. 47 (1932) 137–43.

Maxwell, Constantia, 'Edmund Spenser: The Poet in Exile (1580–

1598)', in *The Stranger in Ireland: From the Reign of Elizabeth to the Great Famine* (London: Jonathan Cape, 1954) pp. 20–37.

Moore, C., 'Spenser's Knowledge of the Neighbourhood of Mitchelstown', *Journal of the Cork Historical and Archaeological Society*, vol. 10 (1904) 31–3.

O'Laidhin, T. (ed.), *Sidney State Papers* (Dublin: Irish Manuscripts Commission, 1962).

'Pedigree of the Poet Spencer's Family', *Journal of the Cork Historical and Archaeological Society*, vol. 12 (1906) facing p. 197.

Plomer, H. R., 'Edmund Spenser's Handwriting', *Modern Philology*, vol. 21 (1923) 201–7.

Pollen, J. H., 'The Irish Expedition of 1579', *The Month*, vol. 101 (1903) 69–85.

Read, Conyers, 'Review of *The Life of Edmund Spenser*, by Alexander C. Judson', *American Historical Review*, vol. 51(3) (1946) 538–9.

Renwick, W. L. (ed.), *A View of the Present State of Ireland* (London: Scholartis Press, 1934).

Smith, Roland M., 'Spenser, Holinshed, and the *Leabhar Gabhala*', *Journal of English and Germanic Philology*, vol. 43 (1944) 390–401.

——, 'Spenser's Scholarly Script and "Right Writing"', in D. C. Allen (ed.), *Studies in Honor of T. W. Baldwin* (Urbana: University of Illinois Press, 1958) pp. 66–111.

'Spenser in Ireland: Review of Pauline Henley, *Spenser in Ireland* (Cork: Cork University Press, 1928)', *The Times Literary Supplement*, vol. 27 (7 June 1928) 422.

Welply, W. H., 'Spenser in Ireland', *The Times Literary Supplement*, vol. 32 (18 May 1933) 348.

——, 'Edmund Spenser's Brother-in-law, John Travers', *Notes and Queries*, vol. 179 (1940) 70–8, 92–7, 112–15.

White, J. G., *Historical and Topographical Notes on Buttevant, Castletownroche, Doneraile, Mallow, and places in their vicinity*, 4 vols (Cork, 1905–16).

Wilson, F. P., 'Spenser and Ireland', *Review of English Studies*, vol. 2 (1926) 456–7.

Index